STUDENT UNIT GUIDE

NEW EDITION

OCR A2 Economics Unit F585
The Global Economy

John Hearn

PHILIP ALLAN

Philip Allan Updates, an imprint of Hodder Education, an Hachette UK company, Market Place, Deddington, Oxfordshire OX15 0SE

Orders
Bookpoint Ltd, 130 Milton Park, Abingdon, Oxfordshire OX14 4SB
tel: 01235 827827
fax: 01235 400401
e-mail: education@bookpoint.co.uk
Lines are open 9.00 a.m.–5.00 p.m., Monday to Saturday, with a 24-hour message answering service. You can also order through the Philip Allan Updates website: www.philipallan.co.uk

ISBN 978-1-4441-7203-4

First printed 2012
Impression number 5 4 3 2 1
Year 2016 2015 2014 2013 2012

Cover photo: Ingram

Typeset by Integra Software Services Pvt. Ltd., Pondicherry, India

Printed in Dubai

Hachette UK's policy is to use papers that are natural, renewable and recyclable products and made from wood grown in sustainable forests. The logging and manufacturing processes are expected to conform to the environmental regulations of the country of origin.

P2133

Contents

Getting the most from this book

Questions & Answers

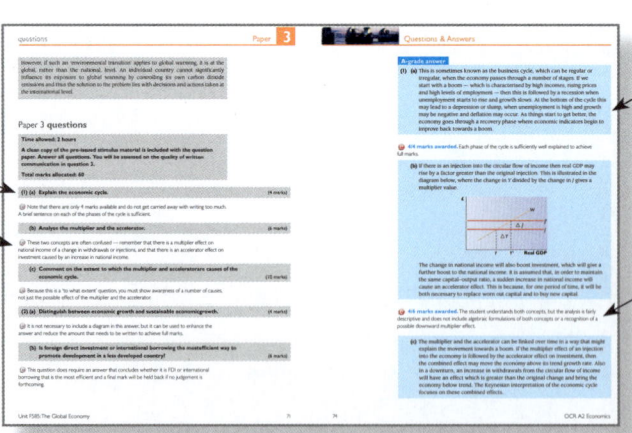

About this book

From the very start of your A2 course it is necessary to grasp the difference between the synoptic unit and other units studied to complete the AS so that you do not involve yourself in unnecessary work, but focus clearly on the essential elements required to be successful in this examination.

The **Content Guidance** section offers a broad overview of Unit F585: The Global Economy, and its four main areas of study:

- macroeconomic performance
- trade and integration
- development and sustainability
- the economics of globalisation

For each study area, there is a clear statement regarding the skills that must be developed. By the time of the examination, you must have learnt the definitions of a number of key words and be able to understand certain concepts, hypotheses and theories, many of which are drawn from the AS specification.

An attempt has been made to highlight the most relevant parts from the units already studied, but remember that you may be questioned on any part of the AS specification. Understanding on its own is not enough, so the Content Guidance also identifies the things you need to be able to explain, analyse, apply and evaluate within a European context in order to achieve a high grade.

Fundamental to macroeconomic performance is an understanding of economic growth. In consequence, the emphasis throughout the first section is on what is meant by economic growth, its causes, its consequences and its effect upon the other main targets of government macroeconomic policy, as well as the degree to which it has been actioned over recent years.

For much of the twentieth century, China tried to isolate itself from the rest of the world and be self-sufficient. Despite having one fifth of the world's population, its economy was stagnant and its people were destined for a life of poverty with little hope that living standards would improve over their lifetime. However, as we moved into the twenty-first century, China embraced change. It became a global player, trading throughout the world, and suddenly it saw an explosion of economic growth and rising standards of living. The second section in this unit looks at how international trade and the gradual integration of national economies has benefited countries in general.

But, of course, not everything has proceeded without a few problems along the way. Despite significant growth, development and change, there are still considerable differences in the real income and welfare of the richest and poorest countries. The third section looks at growth and development throughout the world, particularly in the less developed countries, with a view to examining strategies for promoting economic development. Again, this requires a measure to determine the success of those strategies and an understanding of the limits to change. We will also consider whether these developments are brief and likely to be reversed in the future or whether they are sustainable into future generations.

With the internet speeding up the flow of information, travel becoming more affordable, China opening up and India taking a more outward and forward-looking approach, the world is becoming a global market. The last section in this unit looks at globalisation and its impact on the world economy.

The **Questions & Answers** section of this guide includes three sets of case study materials, equivalent to those that would be pre-issued by the examining board. Following this are the three related examination papers, which include questions, a mark scheme and an A-grade answer that students might make.

This unit will probably be the last one studied to complete the OCR A-level specification. It carries 25% of the overall marks and, like the other chosen A2 unit, its assessment is synoptic, which means that it will have built upon the knowledge and understanding of work covered in the AS units.

By the time you start to study this unit, you will be aware that much of the economic theory you have learnt is being used again to build more sophisticated theories and to analyse and evaluate more complex situations. In this way, the AS provides stepping stones which lead you closer to understanding the real nature of a national economy, international groupings of countries and the less formal economic ties that bind the global economy.

The importance of keeping up to date

If this book had been written a few years ago, it would have described a world of relatively fast economic growth rates, with countries like China and India booming and the more mature countries of Europe and the USA growing more slowly, but with low rates of inflation, sound money, high levels of employment and satisfactory balances on their external accounts. However, as we moved into the beginning of 2009, the world was suffering a financial crisis, inflation rates having moved above their agreed targets through much of 2008 and then falling rapidly, unemployment was starting to rise and external accounts were more volatile. Governments around the world took action with fiscal stimulus programmes and slightly different versions of quantitative easing. By 2012 deflation had been avoided, but there remains a stubbornly high rate of inflation and relatively low rates of economic growth and high unemployment. The world economy may not be suffering deflation, but it still shows many of the characteristics of recession.

The important point is that changes can take place very quickly in economics and you need to keep up to date. Read a quality newspaper, keep abreast of the news relevant to your studies and dip into various financial websites. Nothing impresses the examiner more than you having set your studies in context in the real world. While all other students are referring to what happened when the textbooks were being written, you should make sure that your economic knowledge is as up to date as the morning of your examination. Always trying to apply your economic knowledge to the real world makes things more interesting for you and therefore makes economics easier to understand and will improve your overall performance.

Pre-issued stimulus material

It may seem something of a contradiction to tell you how important it is to keep up to date when this examination pre-issues stimulus material 6 to 8 weeks before you sit the exam. However, you should take this to be a foundation for your knowledge, but not a limit to your studies.

The way in which you study this unit is very different from the way you study the rest of A-level economics. Before you sit the examination, you will be issued with stimulus material. This may include articles from *Economic Review*, bank reviews, newspapers and other periodicals and occasional papers from various organisations. It may also include sets of statistical data. Some of the factual knowledge required in the examination will be incorporated in the pre-issued material. Although you will not be able to carry notes or any of the case study material into the examination, you will be provided with a clean set of material along with an unseen question paper.

After the case study material has been issued, and before the examination, the sensible approach as you familiarise yourself with the content is to ask yourself (and your teacher) what economic theory learnt in the AS part of the course is directly relevant to what you are currently reading. Although you should not place too much reliance on question-spotting, it would be foolish not to try to anticipate the questions that are likely to be asked and prepare notes on these inspired guesses. For example, if an article is about the rate of economic growth in India or comparative advantage in China or sustainable economic development in Vietnam, then the focus of a significant part of your preparation is set.

Planning your work and preparing a revision strategy

- Familiarise yourself with the specification content included in the AS units.
- From the start of the course, read a quality newspaper and extract all the relevant articles about the economics of Europe.
- Listen to current affairs and news programmes and be prepared to write down relevant points about economic growth, trade and integration, development and sustainability and globalisation.
- Read the relevant articles in *Economic Review* (including back copies), published four times a year by Philip Allan Updates, and current bank reviews.
- The internet provides a range of websites from which information about Europe can be gathered. Any search engine can be a useful starting point. It is now possible to put any single word into the Google search engine and bring up a wealth of information, some of which is likely to be relevant. Wikipedia is a useful online encyclopedia but you need to be careful as it is not as rigorously edited as printed books. Some useful websites are listed below:
  - **www.bankofengland.co.uk**
  - **www.hm-treasury.gov.uk/press**
  - **www.ecb.int** (European Central Bank)
  - **www.worldbank.org** (for worldwide data and maps)

- **www.un.org** (follow the links through 'text version' to 'Cyber School Bus' and 'InfoNation' among a choice of other useful sites)

  Libraries that receive *The Economist* can take advantage of a free subscription to the internet edition, which includes a searchable archive of past articles.

- Be prepared to start work on the pre-issued case study material as soon as it arrives.

- The assessment objectives are weighted heavily to the higher-level skills, so always try to take your preparatory work up to these levels. Level 3 questions will often use the following words:

  account for   consider   analyse   explain   apply   justify   compare

  while level 4 will often use:

  assess   discuss   comment   evaluate   criticise   to what extent?

- As early as possible, find out the date of your examination so that you can prepare a revision strategy. You should include a stock of time that can be used if any emergency should arise.

- Avoid the tendency to revise the material you already know and to ignore the more difficult parts of the course. It is reasonable to assume that the aspects you find difficult are going to appear in the examination as a test of higher-level skills.

- The process of organisation, preparation and revision that goes on throughout the course will have rooted some content firmly in your long-term memory. Over the last few weeks, help your short-term memory to upload the final details by using acronyms to remember lists, patterns to remember links and key words to trigger a series of associated points.

- If time allows, allocate several weeks to work on each of the three practice examination papers included in this guide.

Content Guidance

About 6 weeks before the examination, you will receive pre-issue stimulus material. This will include five or six extracts loosely based around a theme, a country or a group of countries. Although it would be unwise to focus attention only on the extracts, they will provide the context which will guide you through the last weeks of revision.

Because 'The Global Economy' is a synoptic unit, it can draw upon knowledge and understanding from either of the two AS units. It is, however, a macroeconomic unit and therefore you can expect that Unit F582, 'The National and International Economy', will provide essential building blocks. The aggregate demand and supply model may be useful in answering questions, as will the knowledge you have gained about macroeconomic policy objectives, the indicators of national economic performance, the application of policy objectives and the international economy.

Macroeconomic performance

In this unit, the focus in terms of economic performance is on how the UK economy has grown over recent years. Short-run and long-run effects are analysed, as is the effect of various policies and initiatives to promote sustainable growth, relative stability and international competitiveness. Also, an evaluation of the role played by economic growth within the context of other economic objectives will be discussed.

Trade and integration

Almost every economist promotes the benefits of free international trade based upon the theory of comparative advantage. Protectionism can be justified under special circumstances but, in an economically efficient world, should be avoided. There is, however, the temptation — usually for political vote-catching reasons — to consider protecting trade. This is especially the case when the world is moving towards recession and each individual country is seeking to protect itself from the downturn by promoting domestic concerns at the expense of international integration.

Development and sustainability

There is a difference between economic growth and economic development, and there is a target for all forms of improvement to be sustainable. There is also a recognition that, on its own, economic growth does not necessarily equate with improvements in living standards. Therefore wider measures of whether countries are becoming better off or not are made by the human development index rather than just via gross domestic product per capita.

The economics of globalisation

Is the world becoming one enormous global village? Given the imbedded conflicts of interest, can the world ever become one big happy family? There are signs that it can, given that the mobility of people across the world is increasing, communication is now almost instant and shopping in America, Hong Kong, France or Australia can be achieved

without leaving your home, thanks to the internet. Free market forces may stall through periods of economic downturn and people may look to their governments for support and protection, but it is unlikely that the process of globalisation will not continue.

Background knowledge

It is important in economics to know your definitions precisely, along with the theories that underpin the subject. This means that the work covered during the AS course is an important foundation on which to build, and essential definitions must be part of the knowledge you carry forward into studying this unit.

When you receive the stimulus material, it is advisable to read through the extracts and highlight all the underlying economic theory that is referred to, or is implicit within what is written. Then go back to your AS notes and make sure that all the relevant theory is understood. The examining board has made it quite clear that it wants to test whether you can think like an economist and effectively apply the concepts, hypotheses and theories you have learned in the compulsory units.

When you completed the AS course, the emphasis of your studies was on explanation and analysis with some evaluation. In this examination, the emphasis has changed and if you look through the specification content, you will see more than 20 references to evaluation, discussion and comment. These are the higher-level skills which you need to master before you can receive the higher-level marks.

Essential terms

You will need to be able to define and use the following essential terms:

- absolute advantage
- aggregate demand
- aggregate supply
- balance of payments
- circular flow of income
- comparative advantage
- demand management
- economic growth
- exchange rates
- fiscal policy
- gross domestic product
- inflation
- nominal
- real
- supply-side economics
- unemployment

Knowledge check 1

What is the difference between absolute advantage and comparative advantage in international trade?

Macroeconomic performance

At the beginning of 2009, the global economy was in a recession caused by a global credit crunch, which in turn started as the result of over-ambitious banks purchasing securitised packages of sub-prime property mortgages from American lenders. The problem was so large that a number of investment banks in the USA failed and retail banks in the UK were only saved from bankruptcy by government intervention. The main damage throughout the world has been a loss of confidence in the banking system and a contraction of aggregate monetary demand.

In an attempt to alleviate these problems, the Bank of England reduced the bank rate to a record low of 0.5% in March 2008. At the beginning of 2009, the rate of inflation, which had risen to 5% during 2008, fell back sharply to 3.1% (consumer price index) in January 2009. The Bank of England's target for inflation was 2%, so even though it had fallen quickly, it was still above target. However, the main concern was with the rate of reduction coupled with a recession being measured officially by a decline in real GDP over two successive quarters. In the third quarter of 2008, GDP declined by 0.6% and in the fourth quarter, at the even faster rate of 1.5%.

By December 2008, the claimant count measure of unemployment had risen to 1.16 million, while the ILO measure was at 1.92 million. The balance of payments current account deficit for the year 2007 was £39.5 billion, while the third quarter of 2008 had registered a deficit of £7.7 billion. Large deficits of this order mean the exchange rate is overvalued and, without the protection of higher rates of interest in the UK to attract foreign currency through the financial account of the balance of payments, the exchange rate declined sharply. In August 2008, £1 bought nearly $2 or €1.3. By January 2009, it only bought $1.37 and a little more than €1. This is not all bad news, as export prices will fall and encourage sales, while import prices will rise and discourage purchases.

In 2009 the government started on a fiscal and monetary expansion. Along with the other G20 countries the UK budgeted for a large deficit reaching £179 billion for the fiscal year 2009/10. It also started a **quantitative easing** (QE) programme which bought back government debt and increased cash liquidity by £200 billion in 2009. This increased to £325 billion in 2012.

As well as having knowledge of actual events, it is essential that you understand and can apply the underlying theory to your analysis and evaluation of global events. The theme of this unit is how the economies of the world are growing and changing. The first thing is to understand the difference between an economy which is growing from inside the production possibility boundary towards the boundary and an economy which is shifting its boundary outwards. Moving towards the boundary is referred to as growth, short-run growth or actual growth, while shifting the boundary outwards is economic growth, long-run trend growth or potential growth. This is illustrated in Figure 1 by a movement from A to B or a shift to position C.

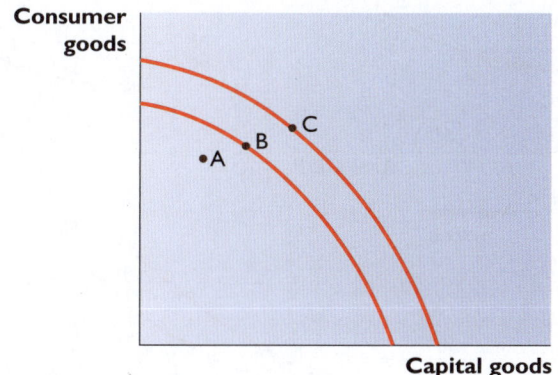

A–B = short-run or actual growth
B–C = long-run economic growth or potential growth

Figure 1

Examiner tip
A recession is defined as occurring when real GDP contracts for two consecutive quarters. It is usually preceded by a boom and is followed by a depression in the economic cycle.

Quantitative easing (QE) This is a process whereby the Bank of England increases liquidity in the economy, usually by buying back outstanding government debt in exchange for cash, hence a common description of QE is that it is printing money.

Examiner tip
Just before you sit the examination, make sure you use the internet to update all of the statistics given here. Should you then need to refer to the current macroeconomic performance of the UK, the examiner will be impressed by your attempt to keep up to date.

Knowledge check 2
An increase in output along which axis in Figure 1 is most likely to bring about economic growth?

The causes of actual growth in the short run will tend to be associated with increases in aggregate demand and its multiplier effect on GDP, as well as the accelerator effect as investment responds to changes in GDP. Remember that it is the multiplier which affects GDP, while it is changes in GDP which cause the accelerator to raise GDP even further. This interaction between the multiplier and accelerator has often been used to help explain the cycle of economic events that tend to lead an economy through boom into recession and depression and then back to a recovery.

In the long run, potential economic growth is more closely linked to shifts outward in the aggregate supply curve. This is consistent with the definition of economic growth as an increase in per capita productive capacity. It occurs as the result of intervention, innovation and changes in the quality and quantity of the factors of production.

As economic growth is only one of four main macroeconomic targets, it is necessary to evaluate how its pursuit may affect inflation, employment levels and the main balances on the external account.

To achieve its macroeconomic targets and encourage the economy to grow, the government has a range of policies it can use. These can be broadly divided into:
- fiscal policy
- monetary policy
- exchange rate policy
- supply-side policies

The emphasis of fiscal, monetary and exchange rate policies is on promoting actual growth from inside the production possibility frontier towards the boundary. This is illustrated in Figure 2 (i) by shifting the aggregate level of monetary demand to the right, AD to AD^1. In addition to this, the main emphasis of supply-side policies is to shift the aggregate supply curve to the right, AS to AS^1 in Figure 2 (ii), and raise potential economic growth.

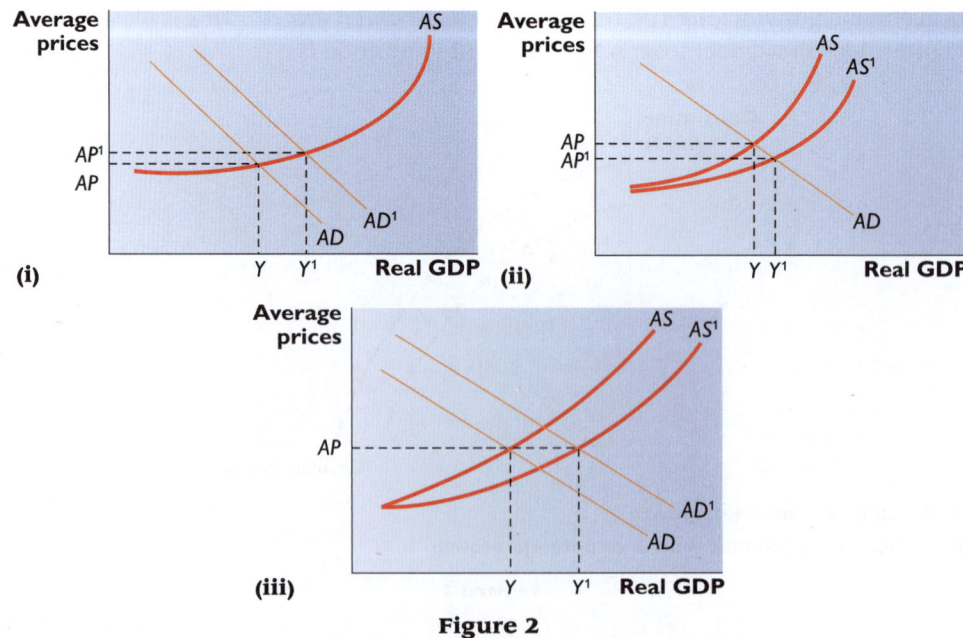

Figure 2

In Figure 2 (ii), you will notice the potential for deflation. In order to avoid this, the ideal response would be a further shift to the right in aggregate demand, as illustrated in Figure 2 (iii).

Although this seems easy to achieve in theory, it is not easy in reality as the actual values for the multiplier and accelerator are not known precisely, and even when fiscal rules are in place they are not met.

- The golden rule is that the government should only borrow to finance capital spending.
- The sustainable (investment) rule is that the public-sector debt should be less than 40% of GDP over the economic cycle.

The above rules have been imposed domestically, while the two rules below form part of the European Union's Stability and Growth Pact for member countries:

- An annual budget deficit should be no higher than 3% of GDP.
- National debt ought to be less than 60% of GDP.

Just before the exam, check to see how well countries are doing in regard to these rules.

Another point to note is that it is possible to refer to fiscal and monetary policies which have supply-side intent. For example, government expenditure on research and development or improvements in infrastructure may shift the aggregate supply curve, as may a reduction in bank rate, which encourages more investment in plant and machinery.

A final point is to recognise that when you use the AD/AS model, there is an interpretation by Keynesians that there is a range over which increases in aggregate demand will increase **real GDP**. The monetarists, in contrast, argue that in the long run, there is a natural level of unemployment (output) and the aggregate supply curve is vertical. This means that increases in aggregate demand will only raise prices and leave output unchanged. If the monetarist/classical argument is correct, then it is only rightward shifts in the aggregate supply curve that can increase real GDP.

Essential terms

You will need to be able to define and use the following essential terms:

- accelerator
- actual growth
- balance of payments current account/capital account/financial account
- consumer price index
- economic cycle
- economic stability
- fiscal policy with supply-side intent
- fiscal rules
- golden rule
- inflation targeting
- long-run aggregate supply
- Monetary Policy Committee
- monetary policy with supply-side intent
- multiplier
- natural rate of employment
- potential economic growth
- short-run aggregate supply
- Stability and Growth Pact
- sustainable investment rule

Knowledge check 3

In Figure 2 (ii) how is the potential for deflation illustrated?

Examiner tip

Since 2009 almost all countries in the more developed world have exceeded these targets for budget deficits and national debt. Remember that throughout this section you need to set the UK economy in a global context. This means looking at the UK within the EU and in a wider global economy which may cover interactions with both more and/or less developed economies.

Real GDP This is the total value of output in an economy adjusted for inflation. It is usually identified by measuring output at constant prices from a chosen base year.

Examiner tip

Fiscal policy with supply-side intent involves looking at the budget from the point of view of not changing the overall level of aggregate demand, but rather making adjustments to taxation or expenditure that may help policies such as promoting economic growth or increasing employment. These changes will not result in the overall balance between expenditure and taxation changing.

Explanation

You will need to be able to explain the following:

- the UK's current and recent macroeconomic performance
- the difference between actual growth and potential economic growth
- the causes of economic growth
- the effect of economic growth on other targets, short- and long-term
- the various policies that can be used to promote short-run actual growth and long-run potential growth
- the targets, constraints and rules governing policy and the trade-offs that may have to take place

Analysis

You need to be able to analyse the following:

- the factors that have affected the recent UK economic performance
- the relationship between causes and rates of actual and potential economic growth
- the significance of output gaps
- how the multiplier and accelerator work
- the mechanism for translating macroeconomic policies into actions and results
- the role of targets, rules and constraints

Evaluation

You will need to be able to evaluate the following:

- the relative effectiveness of the causes of short-run and long-run economic growth
- the sustainability of economic growth
- the arguments for and against economic stability and economic growth
- the effectiveness of the major macroeconomic policies and the awareness of the different views held by monetarist, Keynesian, demand-side and supply-side economists
- the significance and effectiveness of targets, rules and constraints

Check points

Be aware of the following points:

- Remember that there is considerable difference between the theory and reality of economic management. For example, it is not possible to calculate precisely the multiplier effect of an injection or withdrawal from the circular flow of income.
- There is a conflict between the pursuit of policy and macroeconomic targets. For example, a policy to promote growth may benefit employment but damage the current account of the balance of payments and increase the risk of inflation.
- There is a fundamental disagreement between monetarists and Keynesians. Monetarists, because of their understanding of theory, will tend to promote stability through monetary policy and economic growth through supply-side policies or demand-side policies with supply-side intent. Keynesians, on the other hand, will argue for an active fiscal policy and an accommodating monetary policy.

- Macroeconomic performance refers to how the economy as a whole acts and reacts as part of a global economy.
- Here the specification concentrates mainly on economic development and economic growth in the short and long run and how these concepts link to the other main macroeconomic targets of government.
- Fluctuating around a growing economy is an economic cycle of boom, recession, depression and recovery. As the economy grows so each boom is at a higher point and each depression is not quite as low as the last one.

- The multiplier measures the impact investment has on real national income while the accelerator measures the impact on investment of a change in national income.
- The economy can be managed by demand-side policies that shift the aggregate demand curve to the right or by supply-side policies that shift the aggregate supply curve to the right or by a combination of both.
- The extent to which internal macroeconomic policies can affect international competitiveness is important.

Trade and integration

The case for free trade is based upon the theory of comparative advantage. The easiest way to show that you understand this is to illustrate your answer with a theoretical example, where:
- one country has absolute advantage in the production of two products
- opportunity costs are different (remember that if they are the same, there can be no gains from trade)
- by rearranging production through specialisation, the output of both products can be increased

Suppose country A can produce a combination of 5Y and 10Z, while at the same time country B can produce 100Y and 60Z, then we would have:

	Product Y	Product Z
Country A	5	10
Country B	100	60
Total	105	70

Are opportunity costs different?

	Opportunity cost of producing 1Y	Opportunity cost of producing 1Z
Country A	2Z	½Y
Country B	3/5Z	5/3Y

Yes, opportunity cost is different, so if each country specialises by producing more of the product for which it has the lower opportunity costs, then both countries will gain from trade. If country A allocates all its resources to producing product Z and produces 20Z and no Y; and country B produces 10 more Y and 6 less Z, then total output of Y increases to 110 and Z to 74.

Knowledge check 5

Construct a table which shows that country A has absolute advantage in the production of Y and Z and there is no comparative advantage.

Examiner tip

In any two by two matrix, opportunity costs will always be the inverse of each other, e.g. 7/3 and 3/7 or 9/13 and 13/9. If they are not in your work then you have made a mistake.

	Y	Z
Country A	0	20
Country B	110	54
Total	110	74

From an example like this, you can also use the opportunity costs to show where the terms of trade must be for both countries to benefit. In this case, 1Y must trade for a quantity which lies between 3/5Z and 2Z. This is the same as saying 1Z must trade for between ½Y and 5/3Y.

If trade takes place on the limit, or outside the limits to exchange, then only one country will benefit and the other country will lose, or not gain. If the rate is outside the limit, one country will lose; if it is on the limit, then one country will not benefit from trade, but also it will not lose. The preceding example relates to the exchange of two quantities and is therefore illustrating the real terms of trade. Because products have prices which are determined by the interaction of supply and demand in a free market, the actual terms of trade is measured by the formula:

$$\text{Terms of trade} = \frac{\text{index number for the average price of exports}}{\text{index number for the average price of imports}} \times 100$$

A rise in the terms of trade is described as a favourable movement, because with the same sales revenue from selling exports, a country could finance the purchase of more imports. Similarly, a fall in the terms of trade means that less imports can be purchased from the same value of export sales and this is described as unfavourable. However, favourable movements in the terms of trade can have unfavourable effects on the current account of the balance of payments. If, ceteris paribus, export prices rise and the demand for exports is elastic, then sales revenue will fall and the effect on the current account will be unfavourable. Similarly, if export prices fall then this would be described as an unfavourable movement in the terms of trade, but it would have a favourable effect on the current account.

One of the earliest theories of the exchange rate was the 'purchasing power parity' (ppp) theory, which suggested that exchange rates settle when equivalent amounts of currency have identical purchasing power in their respective countries. The fact that this does not happen led to the discrediting of purchasing power parity as a theory of exchange rates, although it is still a very useful concept when making comparisons between countries. Comparative living standards are more clearly reflected using ppp than they are using exchange rates.

In a free market, the exchange rate is determined by the interaction of supply and demand for a currency. The diagram to illustrate this often causes a problem for students, because they forget that you cannot price a currency without using another foreign currency. A further confusion is that it is demand which determines both the supply (demand for imports) and demand (demand for exports) of currency to the foreign exchange market, as illustrated in Figure 3.

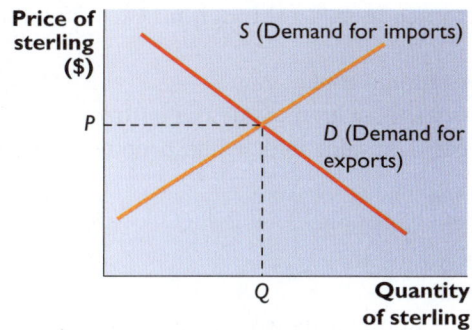

Figure 3

One further assumption regarding the diagram that is usually drawn to determine a free market price for a currency is that, for the supply curve to slope upwards from left to right, the demand for imports must be elastic. For shifts in the demand or supply of currency, you are looking for reasons why more or less currency is supplied or demanded at the same exchange rate. As well as the obvious increase or decrease in the demand for imports and exports, one other important determinant of exchange rates is the rate of interest. When the rate is higher in the UK relative to other countries, demand for UK assets, and therefore demand for sterling, will shift to the right and vice versa.

Exchange rate systems tend to vary between the two extremes of freely floating and fixed. The advantages of a freely floating rate are:

- market forces require prices to adjust to market conditions and a free market does it best
- currencies cannot become significantly over or undervalued
- currency **speculation** is limited

The advantages of a fixed rate are:
- it provides stability for international trade
- it imposes a monetary discipline on government
- speculators benefit when currencies become significantly over or undervalued

When currencies float up and down, the correct terminology to use is appreciation and depreciation. However, when currencies are fixed and they have become over or undervalued, then they may have to be revalued or devalued.

A further point about fixed exchange rate systems is that the rate is determined by market forces in the same way that floating rates are. The only difference is that a government has made an overt statement to maintain the rate at a par value, with slight changes either way, before it will have to intervene by buying the currency when it is falling below its target and selling the currency when it is rising above target.

For most countries on a floating system, such as the UK, it is not a free market float but a managed float, where governments may intervene (covertly) to encourage the currency in one direction or another in pursuit of a particular policy.

In the case of the UK, it is necessary to consider whether to join the single currency (euro) of the European Union. The advantages of doing this include:
- it is estimated that there will be an efficiency gain from removing exchange rate uncertainty and risk

Examiner tip

Differential interest rates between the UK and other countries can have significant distorting effects on the rate of exchange as the flow of currency into and out of a country to make asset purchases is much larger than the flow of funds required to finance trade in goods and services over a given period of time.

Speculation The process of buying and selling assets in the present only to reverse the process in the future and make a profit on a change in the value of an asset.

Examiner tip

This type of managed float is often referred to as a dirty float as it may be used to try to create an unfair advantage that does not reflect true market conditions.

- it will create greater price stability through no exchange rate and one monetary authority
- it is a benefit to international trade
- it will remove currency speculation inside the eurozone
- it would mean joining a system which has a better track record at controlling inflation
- it would impose discipline on the fiscal policy of all member countries

The disadvantages are:
- transition can be costly
- countries are unable to pursue their own monetary policies, having significant limitations on fiscal policy
- unemployment may result, with no option to reflate and devalue currency
- there is a problem of deciding at what rate to enter the system so as to avoid permanently fixing at too low or too high a rate
- it is uncertain whether people would be happy to trade in euros

Examiner tip

The problems highlighted in the eurozone during 2011/12 were to do with the fact that member countries were forced into an agreed monetary policy but allowed to fix their own fiscal budgets. Countries like Greece, Italy and Spain significantly deviated from the agreed stability and growth pact rules for fiscal harmony and destabilised the euro as a currency.

If the UK stays *out* of the eurozone then, in order to correct imbalances in the current account of the balance of payments, it will still be able to reflate or deflate domestic aggregate demand, or support an appreciation or depreciation in the external value of the currency. In addition to this, the UK can adopt other protectionist measures using:
- tariffs
- quotas
- subsidies to domestic industry
- legislation
- differential tax rates
- quality control
- minimum standards
- 'Buy British' campaigns

Knowledge check 7

Why do infant industries need to be protected?

The case for protection includes:
- infant industries can be supported
- senile industries can be maintained while they regenerate
- unfair trading practices, such as dumping and foreign monopoly suppliers, can be countered
- there is protection against illegal imports, e.g. drugs
- national security is easier to maintain
- it provides a source of government revenue

The case against protection includes:
- protection could become permanent, rather than just being a temporary misallocation of resources
- infant industries may never grow up
- there could be retaliation from foreign countries
- it could raise the cost of living
- consumer choice might be limited
- it ignores the benefits from comparative advantage

There is a knock-on effect when one country imposes a restriction on international trade; it leads to other individual countries protecting themselves in a way that gives no real benefits either to themselves or to anyone else and imposes a misallocation of resources within the global economy. The result has been that, over more recent years, countries have reached different levels of economic integration with other countries. These have included:

- free trade areas, where a group of countries agree to trade freely with each other but maintain a protective barrier against the rest of the world
- customs unions, where countries not only agree to trade freely with each other, but agree a common external barrier against the rest of the world
- economic unions, where the group of countries integrate not only their trade but also their policies and laws, allowing the free flow of productive factors as well as products
- monetary union, where the economic union chooses to adopt a single currency to facilitate trade and integration

Economic integration allows individual countries to benefit from the theory of comparative advantage and to specialise in the production of goods for which they have lower opportunity costs. The transition can often be difficult while resources are reallocated in a more efficient way. Pockets of unemployment may result as the benefits from greater efficiency are not spread evenly and, until the global economy becomes one big economic and monetary union, there will still be distortions caused by different currencies and levels of protection.

Essential terms

- absolute advantage
- balance of payments accounts
- comparative advantage
- customs unions
- economic unions
- exchange rates
- fixed exchange rates
- floating exchange rates

- free trade areas
- managed float
- monetary unions
- purchasing power parity
- terms of trade
- **trade creation**
- **trade diversion**
- **trade liberalisation**

Explanation

You will need to be able to explain:

- the difference between absolute advantage and comparative advantage
- how lower opportunity costs lead to specialisation and gains from trade
- the current pattern of global trade
- how exchange rates are determined
- the difference between an exchange rate and a purchasing power parity
- the stages of economic integration

Analysis

You will need to be able to analyse:

- a theoretical example of gains from trade
- the significance of the terms of trade and the relative importance of changes in the terms of trade
- balance of payments disequilibria and the corrective policies that can be used
- exchange rate fluctuations and shifts and movements in supply and demand curves for currencies
- trade creation and trade diversion

Trade creation New trade created by a change in trade barriers between countries.

Trade diversion
Trade lost by a change in trade barriers between countries.

Trade liberalisation
This has taken place when there is an overall net trade creation.

Knowledge check 8

What effect does a fall in exchange rates have on the prices of imports and exports?

Knowledge check 9

Would you choose to appreciate the currency or deflate domestic demand to solve a persistent large deficit on the current account of the balance of payments?

Evaluation

You will need to be able to evaluate:

- whether the theory of comparative advantage reflects the pattern of global trade
- the advantages and disadvantages of various exchange rate systems
- the effectiveness of policies that can be used to correct imbalances on external account
- the cases for and against protection and free trade
- the overall effect on countries of joining supranational groups

Check points

Be aware of the following points:

- Make sure you can explain an example of comparative advantage where one country has absolute advantage in both products.
- Remember that opportunity costs identify who produces what and the limits between which the terms of trade will settle.
- Note that favourable movements in the terms of trade can have favourable or unfavourable effects on the balance of payments.
- Consider the global effects of moving towards free trade and the effect of a global recession on this movement.

Summary

- An improvement in the terms of trade can worsen the current account of the balance of payments as relatively higher prices for exports reduce revenues from exports and increase expenditure on imports. The opposite happens with a worsening of the terms of trade.
- The European Union (EU) includes all the countries of the eurozone as well as those countries that were originally members of the EU but did not join the eurozone; the UK is one example of the latter.
- A continuing large external account deficit on the current account of the balance of payments is an indication that a country's exchange rate is overvalued relative to the currencies of those countries which make up its trading partners.
- Economic integration makes sense in economic terms, but sometimes imposes significant pressures on member countries that may outweigh the economic benefits.

Development and sustainability

Economic development The process of raising real per capita income with a view to improving people's standard of living.

It is reasonable to assume that economic growth is a necessary, though not sufficient, condition to ensure **economic development**. Economic growth is a fairly narrow definition which states that there must be an increase in productive capacity per capita. This can happen if a government introduces a new way of producing nuclear warheads, but most people would not consider this a necessary condition for development — in fact, the very opposite. In September 2000 the United Nations agreed the following goals, known as the Millennium Development Goals:

- eradicate extreme poverty and hunger
- achieve universal primary education
- promote gender equality
- reduce child mortality

- improve maternal health
- combat HIV/AIDS, malaria and other diseases
- ensure environmental sustainability
- develop a global partnership for development

Measuring anything and expecting it to show something precisely is fraught with danger. Despite its limitations, the most common measure of growth and economic growth is to use real GDP per capita, which is simply the total output of the economy divided by the number of people in the country.

In 1972, W. Nordhaus and J. Tobin attempted to create a wider measure of economic welfare (MEW). It included gross national product plus a value for production in the informal economy, leisure time, deductions for environmental damage and travel time to work.

In 1990, the United Nations devised a fuller measure, to include not only GDP per capita but also a measure of literacy and school enrolment as well as life expectancy. This human development index is the most commonly referred to measure of development, although the Friends of the Earth developed the idea further with its index of sustainable economic welfare (ISEW), and tried to measure genuine increases in the quality of life with additions for unpaid household labour and deductions for air pollution, income inequality and a wider interpretation of environmental damage and depletion of resources.

In 2005, the United Nations identified 137 countries or areas as less developed countries (LDCs). Between the LDCs and the more developed world were 27 other economies identified as transition economies, mainly in eastern Europe. The divisions are not fixed in stone and various countries, such as Singapore and South Korea, should probably be described as more developed countries.

There is a broad division between the northern and southern halves of the globe, with the more developed countries — generally speaking — in the northern hemisphere and the less developed in the southern hemisphere. A further sub-division of LDCs is into three groups. The first comprises Southeast Asian countries like Singapore, Hong Kong (China) and South Korea, which have grown rapidly over recent years and been referred to as newly industrialised countries (NICs), or tiger economies. The second grouping is in sub-Saharan Africa where, as yet, there are no success stories and many countries are the poorest of the less developed countries. The final group is in Latin America where growth, after an initial burst, stalled and was damaged by excessive inflation, balance of payments problems and an unstable currency.

This diversity means that only some of the causes of low growth and third world status can be applied to individual countries. The characteristics of these countries include:
- high population growth
- higher birth and death rates
- lower average age
- higher levels of illiteracy
- few middle income earners
- high concentrations of workers employed in primary industry
- low skill levels
- subsistence incomes
- undeveloped social infrastructures
- few public and merit goods
- immature financial structure

Examiner tip

Sustainability in terms of environmental actions means using renewable resources at a rate equal to or below their ability to regenerate. Regarding government actions, it means that capital expenditure generates sustainable current expenditure that, at least, produces social benefits that cover social costs.

Knowledge check 10

What is a primary industry?

- unsound currency
- political instability

The causes of these problems may include:
- higher than average population growth
- a lack of natural resources
- little physical capital
- unsound financial structure
- poor social capital
- undeveloped human capital
- cultural inhibitions
- political problems

The solution to these problems may be a growth in trade of primary products, which has the advantage of using traditional skills to provide basic raw materials. However, this has the dual disadvantage of reliance on one product and volatile prices, as supply and demand curves are relatively inelastic.

Alternatively, a growth in trade of manufactured goods could lead to import substitution or export-led growth. Historically, export-led growth seems to have been the more successful choice.

Development through borrowing has its inherent dangers and debt crises have hit many less developed countries when interest rates rose and their sources of income declined.

Development through aid has the problem of creating a dependency culture and is probably best used to overcome emergencies rather than to fund long-term growth.

Foreign direct investment (FDI) by multinational corporations is helping to improve the lot of LDCs. There is official aid through the Overseas Development Assistance (ODA) programme of the OECD. The heavily indebted poor countries (HIPC) initiative, which was set up in 1995, is concerned with debt relief for HIPCs with demonstrable good intentions, while a structural adjustment programme (SAP) is a World Bank initiative to direct poor countries towards development and growth.

So what are the main obstacles to development and growth?

- The demographic transition from high population growth and high death rates to low population growth and low birth rates may be something that happens by itself, creating low and stable population growth. On the other hand, it may be that intervention is necessary to speed up this process.
- There may be a dependency on primary production and out-of-date methods of production, along with confusion over property rights.
- Failure of the merit goods to deal with health problems such as HIV/AIDS and promote the necessary education to improve the quality of human capital is frequently an issue.
- A weak financial system means that customers can have little confidence in the savings and investment opportunities that need to be available in a growing economy.
- Unstable political systems are often more concerned with self interest rather than promoting the structural reforms and public goods which are a necessary pre-requisite of growth and development.

Economic growth and development are considered sustainable if the needs and aspirations of the current generation are met without compromising the expected needs of future generations.

Examiner tip

Politically it is easier to sell a policy that targets import substitution as it actively benefits local producers and consumers. In contrast, export-led growth can be criticised from the point of view that the local workforce is working hard to benefit consumers in other countries.

Examiner tip

A question that is difficult to answer is whether economic growth causes birth rates and death rates to fall or whether it is falling birth rates and death rates that help to promote economic growth.

Over recent years, it has become clearer that countries can also be judged to have environmental capital, the World Heritage sites and the Wonders of the World being obvious examples. Degradation of the environment is damaging biodiversity and causing current and future external costs in a globalised world. These costs are not limited to the countries where the damage is taking place, but spread out to nearby, and in some cases to all, countries. It is difficult to deal with these problems without resorting to international laws and actions.

Over the longer term, the accelerating use of non-renewable resources will change the patterns of production and consumption while, at the same time, making some countries rich in the present but impoverished in the future.

One attempt to value degradation is by measuring the carbon footprint:
- A primary footprint measures carbon dioxide emissions from energy consumption and transportation.
- A secondary footprint is an indirect measure of carbon dioxide emissions through the whole life cycle of products and waste disposal.

The Kyoto Protocol has established targets and timetables for the reduction of greenhouse emissions. It is encouraging carbon offsetting activities, such as tree planting, and is attempting to promote awareness of the footprint through the Carbon Trust.

Essential terms

- absolute poverty
- biodiversity
- carbon footprint
- environmental capital
- environmental degradation
- export-led growth
- heavily indebted poor countries (HIPC)
- human development index (HDI)
- import-led growth
- index of sustainable economic welfare (ISEW)
- less developed countries (LDCs)
- Millennium Development Goals
- measure of economic wealth (MEW)
- Organisation for Economic Co-operation and Development (OECD)
- Overseas Development Assistance (ODA)
- relative poverty
- sustainable economic growth/ development
- structural adjustment programme (SAP)
- tiger economies

Explanation

You will need to be able to explain the following:
- the difference between growth and development
- how economic growth is an important component of economic development
- the similarities and differences between different countries as they develop
- what is meant by sustainable economic growth/development

Analysis

You will need to be able to analyse the following:
- the usefulness of measures such as GDP and HDI for measuring economic development
- the usefulness of measures such as MEW and ISEW in measuring sustainability
- the various causes and effects of growth at the various stages of development

Examiner tip

The price mechanism has a part to play in allocating non-renewable resources in a more efficient way. As prices rise, so fewer resources will be used and more alternative ways of producing the same products will be developed.

Knowledge check 11

What points should be included in a definition of 'standard of living'?

Examiner tip

If you are required to make any points of discussion then make sure you keep up to date with the arguments surrounding global warming and environmental degradation, especially where scientists have been questioned over the reliability of the statistics upon which they have based some of their predictions.

Evaluation

You will need to be able to evaluate the following:

- the effectiveness of the various policies and agreements, national and international, that have been and are being used to encourage development
- the importance of international trade and further economic integration in encouraging development
- the constraints on development and how they vary from one country to another and from inside and outside the country
- whether the policy makers can rely on the various measures and indicators of economic development when formulating strategies

Check points

Be aware of the following points:

- Although there are similarities, each country is unique and the characteristics and causes of its problems and their solutions need to be tailor-made.
- There is no one-size-fits-all approach to economic development that will solve problems, although there are common themes throughout groups of countries that can be a target for growth and development.
- Sustainability and the science that underpins it is still evolving and may change attitudes as we become more aware of environmental degradation.

Summary

- Economic development is the all-embracing concept which includes narrowly-defined economic growth as well as all those factors that make up a country's standard of living.
- If required by the question it is necessary to be critical of all the measures of an economy's growth, development and sustainability. They all have their strengths and weaknesses and none of them is definitive.
- Solutions to the problems of low growth and third world status will vary from one country to another and trying to superimpose one country's success story on to another is unlikely to be successful and may even damage the country in question.
- We are rich because you are poor is often an underlying assumption of the uneven distribution of wealth and income around the world. This is a beggar-my-neighbour view of international trade that is not supported by the economic analysis of comparative advantage.

The economics of globalisation

The economics of globalisation is ever changing so make sure you keep up to date with the changes that take place daily. A good website and a quality newspaper should keep you informed.

Products move ever more quickly. Across the world, people communicate face to face over the internet. Ideas flow around the globe on a communication network that is not controlled by any one country and finance passes across international borders without restriction. This economic integration on a worldwide scale is now commonly referred to as globalisation.

The causes of the globalisation process are:
- cheaper transport costs for people and products
- cheaper communication costs, in some cases down to zero if the internet is used
- an official reduction in trade barriers and an unofficial reduction where trade is difficult to police
- an increasing number of multinational corporations (MNCs) worldwide due to economies of scale and scope
- a freer flow of financial capital due to deregulation of financial markets

The benefits of globalisation include:
- greater efficiency through economic growth and development
- the alleviation of poverty and some movement towards equality
- a level playing field in trade where international law and rules are equally applied
- arguably, more tolerance and less conflict as increased communication causes greater awareness

The costs of globalisation include:
- externalities are of particular concern where MNCs are expanding in countries with lax environmental controls
- exclusion and conflict may be felt as people become more aware of the relative uneven distribution of income and wealth across the world
- crime and a loss of political control have led to more identity theft, money laundering and scams that are a significant cost to economies throughout the world
- anti-globalisation protests are based upon the lowering of environmental standards and the expected uneven benefits of globalistion that may make the rich richer, while failing to benefit the poorer countries

The financial account of the balance of payments measures the flow of financial assets into and out of a country or group of countries. Private investment flows and official central government transactions are included, as well as changes in foreign exchange reserves.

A relatively small account on the balance of payments is the capital account, which measures capital transfers, often via resident migrants sending money abroad and other physical transfers of ownership.

Multinational corporations (MNCs) engage in **foreign direct investment (FDI)** in LDCs for many reasons, the main ones being:
- increased efficiency and profits
- improved access to markets
- nearness to productive factors such as raw materials or labour with particular skills

The benefits of FDI include:
- improved human capital
- support services will be required
- solving of unemployment problems
- creation of a source of tax revenue
- increases in real disposable income

Examiner tip
Globalisation is taking place and will continue to take place as long as communications between countries become easier and less restricted. However, any analysis of globalisation needs to recognise that this process has its costs and benefits. Economic theory suggests that the benefits will always outweigh the costs in total, but the net benefits will not always be equitably distributed.

Examiner tip
Within the financial account of the balance of payments are the official transactions that take place to produce an overall zero balance. These include changes to the foreign exchange reserves and official borrowing and lending in foreign currency.

Foreign direct investment (FDI) This involves taking over the ownership of productive assets in another country. It is then likely to bring about an improvement in the skills and expertise of the enterprise in the host country.

The costs of FDI include:

- exploitation of productive factors
- tendency to be capital intensive and creating few local jobs
- ability to get away with reduced environmental protection legislation and therefore create more pollution
- taking profits out of the country
- possible damage to local firms

The World Trade Organization (WTO) is concerned with reducing trade barriers and promoting free trade and global investment.

The International Monetary Fund (IMF) was at its peak of influence when the world traded under the gold exchange standard and currencies were fixed against each other. Today it is less important, but it is still concerned with helping countries which get into short-term difficulties to finance their balance of payments.

The World Bank was formerly known as the International Bank for Reconstruction and Development. Its role is to provide long-term funding for projects in creditworthy less developed countries, while the International Development Association (IDA) is another part of the World Bank which deals with more risky developments.

Overall, international trade negotiations can be grouped into those that promote market-friendly activities and those that require state planning. Debates centre around market failures and government failures.

The strength of markets is that they encourage competition and growth and motivate the workforce, as long as there are strong regulatory authorities in place to ensure a level playing field. The weaknesses are the external costs and failure to provide public goods and merit goods in sufficient quantities.

The strength of state planning is that funds need to be directed and managed to ensure a more efficient allocation of resources, but it is unlikely that government bodies can replace market signals as a cheap and efficient allocative process. It is a fact that many of the resources directed towards development have been swallowed up by the bureaucracies that were supposed to supervise their distribution.

Essential terms

You will need to be able to define the following essential terms:

- externalities
- foreign direct investment (FDI)
- globalisation
- government failure
- human capital
- International Monetary Fund (IMF)
- market failure
- market-friendly growth
- multinational corporations (MNCs)
- Overseas Development Assistance (ODA)
- state planning
- World Bank
- World Trade Organization (WTO)

Examiner tip

The World Trade Organization (WTO) replaced GATT in 1995 with a wider brief to regulate the world trading environment, reduce tariff barriers and help to resolve international trade disputes. It has been reasonably successful in reducing trade barriers on manufactured goods, but has been much less successful at dealing with trade restraints surrounding agricultural products and commodities.

Knowledge check 12

What is the difference between the World Bank and the International Monetary Fund (IMF)?

Explanation

You will need to be able to explain the following:

- the characteristics of globalisation
- the roles of the World Trade Organization, International Monetary Fund and World Bank, including the International Bank for Reconstruction and Development and the International Development Association
- the main international flows of currency and capital

Analysis

You will need to be able to analyse the following:

- the factors which are pushing the globalistion process
- what affects the amount and direction of flows of international finance
- international trade negotiations and current trade disputes

Evaluation

You will need to be able to evaluate the following:

- the advantages and disadvantages of multinational corporations and foreign direct investments
- whether globalisation is an overall benefit to the world economy
- the effect of policies designed to alleviate poverty, and finance designed to promote development

Check points

Be aware of the following points:

- The global recession of 2009 has, according to a World Bank report, pushed 46 million more people below the poverty line, i.e. having less than $1.25 a day to live on. This raises the total below the poverty line to more than 250 million people.
- Is the global recession of 2009 likely to reverse the process of globalistion as countries try to protect their domestic markets from competition by raising trade barriers?
- Is it markets or political and quasi-political organisations that will create greater wealth and a more equitable income distribution throughout the world?

Examiner tip

The global recession of 2009 continued on through to, at least, 2012 as central banks and governments struggled to get to grips with large budget deficits that had little effect on employment and growth, and monetary expansions that seem to have done little more than fuel inflation.

Summary

- Despite what they may preach governments are not the greatest supporters of globalisation as it dissipates their domestic powers and creates a more integrated world where responsibilities are judged on a world scale rather than at a national level.
- There are now multinational companies (MNCs) that are larger in terms of their internal budgets than the budgets of many national economies. This creates a problem as MNCs can negotiate with governments and establish the best terms for their company rather than for any country.
- The debate goes on about whether it is markets that will create the wealth that benefits people across the world or enlightened governments.

Questions & Answers

How to use this section

In this section of the guide there are three samples of pre-issued case study materials and three examination papers, each followed by a mark scheme, a sample A-grade answer and a list of potential problems.

Pre-issued case study materials

Articles and statistics similar to these will be pre-issued 6 or 7 weeks before the exam, and it is important to use the practice materials in this guide as if you are preparing for a real examination. You will not be allowed to take the materials into the examination, but a clean set will be provided with the examination paper.

Questions

In the examination, all the questions are compulsory and the time allocated for answering them is 2 hours. The questions can be drawn from theory and practice that were introduced throughout the AS specification, as well as common themes that can be tested in either of the A2 optional papers. The examination will test the range of assessment objectives, with a heavier weighting on the higher-level skills of application, analysis and evaluation. After each question there is some guidance regarding how the question should be interpreted (shown by the icon ⓔ).

Mark schemes

These are similar to those an examiner would use to complete the initial marking of a script. Each scheme highlights the points that will score marks. However, they are for guidance and do not necessarily illustrate the only correct interpretation. Some answers may be different and equally valid and would therefore be awarded equal marks. The mark schemes will help you focus your attention on what the examiner is looking for. Do not be tempted to read these mark schemes before you attempt to answer the questions. Use the examination papers as if they were the real thing.

Sample answers and examiner comments

After each examination paper, there is a script that reflects the type of answer required for the award of a grade A. This answer is not perfect, but is sufficient to achieve 80% or more. Throughout the sample answer, examiner comments are included, preceded by the icon ⓔ. These comments reflect the strengths and weaknesses of the answer.

Assessment objectives

The aim of stimulus material is to *stimulate* your thought processes and encourage you to think like an economist. The questions on the examination paper will be based on this material, but you will not be able to answer the questions by simply regurgitating what is in the stimulus material. There are, then, three skills required in this unit:

(1) understanding of the pre-issued material
(2) knowledge of which theories, techniques and concepts from your AS and A2 notes are relevant
(3) the ability to express this understanding as an economist in continuous prose

The examining board separates the assessment objectives into four skill levels. These are illustrated in the table below, using the example of a customs union.

Assessment objective	Skills	Percentage of total mark
Level 1	The ability to understand and express knowledge of the specification content, e.g. the ability to write out a definition of a customs union.	20%
Level 2	The ability to apply this knowledge and understanding critically to real and simulated situations, e.g. the ability to explain the extent to which the European Union is a customs union and explain the situation it replaced and how it differs from other economic unions.	20%
Level 3	The ability to use economic principles to analyse the situation, e.g. using a supply and demand diagram to show how trade creation and trade diversion occur when a customs union is set up.	30%
Level 4	The ability to reflect upon economic arguments, apply economic theory to global issues, evaluate evidence and make informed judgements as an economist, e.g. to what extent do customs unions exist in the world and are they part of opening up or restricting trade in a global economy?	30%

It is important to note that the assessment objectives for A2 units are weighted more heavily towards levels 3 and 4, whereas the AS papers have a 20% weighting on levels 3 and 4 and a 30% weighting on levels 1 and 2.

There are quality of language marks included in the mark scheme for the question indicated with an asterisk. In a question worth 20 marks, approximately 4 marks will be set aside for the quality of written communication. The OCR Approved Specifications state that all the quality of language marks will be achieved when:

Complex ideas are expressed clearly and fluently, using a style of writing appropriate to the complex subject matter. Sentences and paragraphs, consistently relevant, are well structured, using specialist technical terminology where appropriate. There are few, if any, errors of spelling, punctuation and grammar.

This means that if you finish the examination paper with a few minutes to go before 'time up', you should re-read your answer and tidy up the quality of your writing.

Paper 1 **extracts**

Extract 1 **Brazil: a country of the future**

Brazil is a country which holds a great fascination for the rest of the world, though our knowledge of it tends to be restricted to the obvious images of football, carnival, Rio de Janeiro and the Amazon. Brazil's landmass is greater than that of the USA, excluding Alaska. The journey from the western border with Peru to the eastern seaboard is longer than that from London to Moscow, and from the northern to the southern borders is about the same distance as New York to Los Angeles.

Brazil is a country of extreme wealth and poverty, and one which is still classified in economic terms as a developing nation. Yet its importance to the global economy cannot be denied. Its importance in world economic affairs is emphasised by the loan of $30 billion which the International Monetary Fund (IMF) granted to Brazil in 2003, while at the same time refusing one to its neighbour Argentina.

Brazil's potential

Table 1 Highlights of the Brazilian economy

- eighth largest economy
- one of the world's major steel producers
- GDP of over $580 billion
- largest exporter of coffee
- eighth largest car manufacturer
- third largest producer of sugar
- fifth largest arms exporter
- more hydroelectric power than any other nation

Brazil's economic achievements are impressive (see Table 1). With its vast natural resources and a growing industrial base, it would appear to have all the potential to compete with the developed economies of Europe and the USA. However, it has also suffered significantly from key economic problems such as spiralling inflation and massive long-term debt, not to mention deep-rooted corruption in its political systems. There is a favourite saying in Brazil that this is a 'country of the future', but cynics often add 'it always will be'. Whether this is true, or whether Brazil will now, in the twenty-first century, realise its potential as one of the world's largest consumer markets may, for the moment, be down to one man — the president, Luiz Inácio Lula da Silva, popularly known as 'Lula'.

President Lula took office on 1 January 2003. His task is to transform the Brazilian economy, which has been plagued by high inflation and increasing international debts. By 2012 there was a measured success in as much as Brazil had grown to be the sixth largest country in the world by GDP and both inflation and budget deficits had been reduced to more manageable more levels.

The economy and market

Brazil is a land of profound economic contradictions. It industrialised rapidly in the second half of the twentieth century, achieving huge economic growth, and is ranked today as the eighth largest economy in the world. However, this has not improved the lot of the vast majority of Brazilians.

The rapid shift from an agriculture-based economy to an industry-based one had huge implications for the demographic make-up of Brazilian society. There was an enormous peasant migration from the poorest rural areas mainly towards the state and city of São Paulo — a trend which still continues. São Paulo is the economic powerhouse of Brazil, and the third or fourth largest city on earth, depending on which figures you read. The truth is that no one knows how many people live in São Paulo, but estimates range between 18 and 22 million. The state of São Paulo constitutes about one quarter of the Brazilian population and uses 60% of the country's energy to produce two-thirds of its industrial output. The gross domestic product of São Paulo state is larger than that of any other nation in Latin America except Mexico. These statistics only serve to underline the importance of Brazil, and in particular São Paulo, for both domestic and international businesses, which may be seeking to target this potential market.

Extract 2 China's comparative advantage?

Under the World Trade Organization's (WTO's) surveillance mechanism, trade policies and practices of members are reviewed regularly. After its accession to the WTO in December 2001, the first trade policy review of China took place in April 2006. The review recognised that China has taken considerable steps in reforming its economy and in opening up to the world. Reform has led to a remarkable transformation of the Chinese economy. Real economic growth has been at 9% over almost two decades, and the percentage of China's population living below the poverty line declined from 73% in 1990 to 25% in 2007. Trade and investment reforms have resulted in China becoming the world's third largest trader and one of the largest recipients of foreign direct investment (FDI). Trade plays an important role in China's economic growth: in 2005, total trade in goods accounted for around 64% of GDP.

China's economic performance has attracted the attention of many economists worldwide. However, of the numerous papers studying the effect of international trade on economic performance, most focus on the role of imports and the analysis of a country's import regime, including tariffs and non-tariff barriers. Few studies have been conducted on China's export structure or its export policies.

Comparative advantage

One may doubt why there is any need to study a country's export structure, since international trade theory tells us that a country's trade will be based on its

comparative advantage. Suppose for simplicity that the world is composed of just two countries, A and B. Assume that Country A can produce a particular good more cheaply, or that it can produce more of the good than Country B can with the same amount of resources. Country A therefore has an absolute advantage over Country B in producing the good in question. In this scenario, one may imagine that Country A will specialise in producing this good and export it to Country B, while Country B will produce and export other goods.

However, in international trade, what matters is not the absolute cost of production, but rather the opportunity cost, which measures how much is given up of one good to produce a unit of another good. Countries trade not because they have an absolute advantage over others, but because of their relative comparative advantage.

In the Heckscher–Ohlin model of international trade there are two factors of production — labour and capital — and countries may specialise in the production of labour-intensive or capital-intensive goods. In general, a country's comparative advantage will depend on its endowments of the two factors. If a county is relatively well endowed with labour, it will have a comparative advantage in the production of labour-intensive goods. Conversely, if it is relatively well endowed with capital, its comparative advantage will lie with the production of capital-intensive goods. This is sometimes termed the 'Rybczynski effect'.

China is a large, developing country with a population of 1.3 billion, so it is natural to suppose that it has a comparative advantage in the production of labour-intensive goods and that such goods will account for most of its exports. However, this view has been challenged in recent research by Dani Rodrik. Rodrik points out that among manufacturing exports, which accounted for more than 90% of China's merchandise exports in 1994, the share of relatively high technology products was approximately 45% (in 1998 the figure was 27%). These products include various types of machinery, transportation equipment and telecommunications equipment. By contrast, exports of relatively low technology products, such as textiles and clothing, accounted for just 16% of total merchandise exports (down considerably from 23% in 1998). Accordingly, Rodrik concluded that China's 'export bundle is that of a country with an income-per-capita level three times higher than China's. China has somehow managed to latch on to advanced, high-productivity products that one would not normally expect a poor, labour abundant country like China to produce, let alone export.'

Extract 3 Development profile: Country J

Country J has a good strategic location, with a long coastline but with a mountainous interior. It is classified by the World Bank as a middle-income country. In 2004, it had a population of 31 million, of whom some 58% live in urban areas. GDP per capita in 2004 was US$1,678 and over the period 1975–2004, growth of GDP per capita averaged 1.4%. It is ruled as a monarchy and has made a bid for membership of the European Union, although the bid has been received without great enthusiasm.

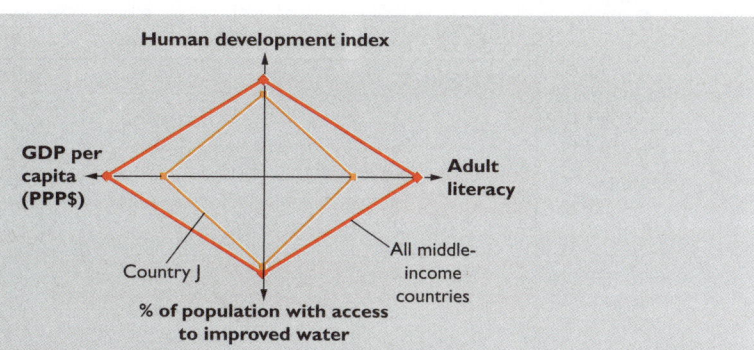

Figure 1 Development diamond comparing Country J with other countries in its region

Figure 1 compares Country J with the average picture for all middle-income countries. As Country J is towards the lower end of the middle income range, it is not surprising to find that it performs below average on most of these items. The fact that Country J performs close to the middle-income average in terms of the percentage of the population with access to improved water is rather ironic, as the World Bank has identified better water management as one of the important challenges facing the country. Droughts are frequent and the agricultural sector uses 92% of all mobilised water in the country. Given current usage rates and projected population growth, it is predicted that water availability per person will be halved by 2020.

Figure 2 shows that Country J has made good and steady progress in human development over the past 30 years. However, Figure 3 is a reminder that poverty and inequality remain a problem within the country. Poverty has been linked with the volatility of the agricultural sector and the effects of drought. In particular, these data reveal a particular issue concerned with gender inequality. Female literacy is only 60% of that for males and female earned income is extremely low compared with men.

There are challenges in the educational sector. School enrolment has improved, but there are still 2.5 million children who are not attending school — many of these being rural girls. Drop-out rates are high and there are problems at tertiary level also. University students take an average of 8 years to complete a 4-year programme, only to find that their skills are unsuited for the labour market.

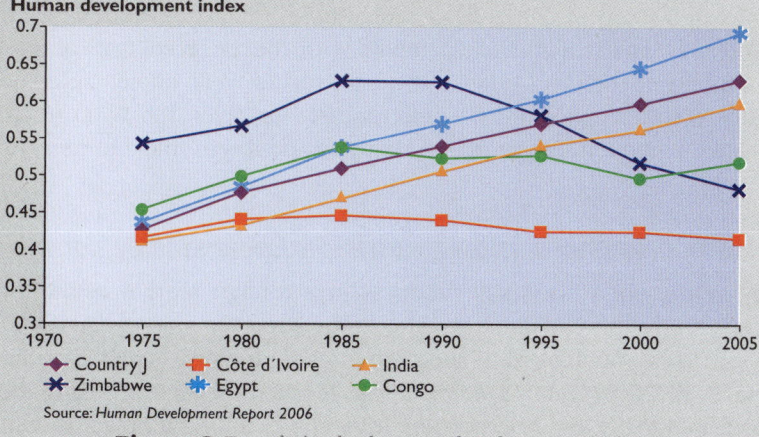

Source: *Human Development Report 2006*

Figure 2 Trends in the human development index

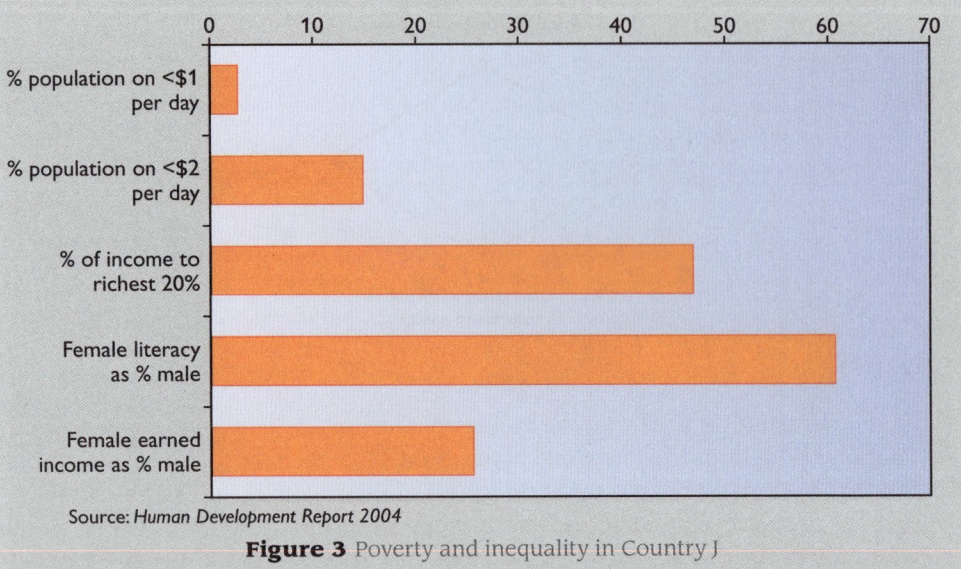

Source: *Human Development Report 2004*

Figure 3 Poverty and inequality in Country J

The performance of Country J in respect of economic growth has been disappointing and unemployment remains high. In 2005, youth unemployment was 17%. The 2000s have brought some improvement, with growth averaging more than 4%, but this is still not enough to bring a swift alleviation of poverty.

Extract 4 US protectionism and China

US protectionist measures

Since China joined the WTO in 2001, the USA has implemented a number of measures designed to limit the flow of Chinese imports into the country.

The imposition of high tariffs on imported steel in 2002

The tariffs imposed varied between 8% and 30% on a range of steel products. This was not targeted solely at China, but affected many countries around the world. The US steel industry was struggling to compete with cheaper steel from abroad and the industry was beset with job losses. The high tariffs were implemented to provide the industry with an opportunity to restructure. However, the WTO ruled that the USA had acted against international trade rules and it was made to remove the high tariffs.

The imposition of anti-dumping tariffs on Chinese televisions in 2004

Dumping occurs when firms sell products in a foreign market below the cost of production. Clearly, this can damage firms in the domestic market and therefore anti-dumping tariffs can be applied to such products if dumping is judged to have taken place. A tariff is a tax on imported products. It has the effect of raising the price of the product, making it less price-competitive and resulting in fewer products being imported. Domestic firms should gain through increased sales, as the quantity of imports is restricted.

The imposition of quota restrictions on Chinese textiles and clothing in 2005

The USA invoked safeguard measures limiting import growth to 7.5% per year for certain goods. These were implemented in an attempt to limit the impact of cheap Chinese products on US firms.

A 27.5% tariff on Chinese imports to the USA

This measure has been proposed but not implemented. Following the huge current account deficit data for 2005, some senators have suggested a 27.5% tariff on Chinese imports if the yuan is not allowed to increase in value further against the dollar.

USA accuses China of dumping cheap solar panels in 2011

Anti-dumping and other investigations into solar panels have denied China access to the lucrative US market.

Extract 5 US protectionism and China

Why is the USA employing protectionist measures?

China's rapid expansion has been mainly export-led. It has been able to take advantage of its ability to:
* produce goods at low cost (primarily because of low wages)
* enter new export markets
* export increasing quantities to existing markets

In 2004, China accounted for 6.5% of world exports and it is in the area of manufactured goods, in particular, that tensions have appeared in the world. China's world share of exports of manufactured goods has almost doubled in just 4 years to 8.25% in 2004.

The World Trade Organization (WTO) also ended its Multi-Fibre Agreement on 31 December 2004. This agreement, established in the 1970s, was created to protect textile industries in industrialised countries from the textile products of low-cost exporting countries. The agreement enabled industrialised countries to set quotas limiting the quantity of textiles entering their country, in order to protect domestic firms and jobs.

As a result of this liberalisation, China has been able to increase its share of global textile sales and has dominated the US market. Of course, this comes at the cost of lost jobs in both developed and developing countries, which are unable to compete with this low-cost giant. Textile firms in the USA have responded by calling for the government to implement 'safeguard measures'. Under the terms of China's entry to the WTO in 2001, countries are allowed to adopt temporary safeguard measures,

which are caps on the quantity of Chinese imports, if the WTO concludes that domestic firms are being hurt by rising Chinese imports.

The US economy has also suffered from a soaring current account deficit. For the past 4 years, it has reached a new record. The deficit was $805 billion in 2005, and represents 7% of gross domestic product. The current account deficit is on an upward trend and by 2011 had grown to $1.07 trillion. Significantly, the deficit with China continues to worsen and indeed, accounts for the largest proportion of the deficit at $216 billion.

Over the past few years, there have been many calls for the Chinese authorities to alter their exchange rate policies. US manufacturers have accused the Chinese authorities of keeping the yuan undervalued and suggest that this has contributed significantly to the US current account deficit, and led to US job losses and the decline of the textiles and electronics industries. They would like the yuan to be revalued or floated freely, so that its rate can be determined by market forces. The Chinese authorities did respond to such calls in July 2005, when the yuan was revalued at 8.11 per dollar. This was 2.1% stronger than its previous level. While this move was welcomed, it was generally held to be too small a revision to have any significant impact on the current account deficit.

Following the latest data on the ever-growing current account deficit, there have been strong calls for further action to revalue the yuan. This would have the effect of making Chinese imports to the USA relatively more expensive and US exports to China more price competitive, hopefully reducing the current account deficit with China.

Paper 1 questions

Time allowed: 2 hours

A clean copy of the pre-issued stimulus materials is included with the question paper. Answer all questions. You will be assessed on the quality of written communication in question 3.

Total marks allocated: 60

(1) (a) Distinguish between actual growth and potential economic growth.   (4 marks)

ⓔ The important thing is to make sure you use comparative statements, i.e. pointing out the distinction between actual growth and potential economic growth. It is not sufficient just to offer definitions of both concepts. It is best to illustrate the distinction by using production possibility boundaries and remembering to label the axes correctly, i.e. capital goods and consumer goods.

(b) Identify macroeconomic policies that can be used to promote both actual and potential economic growth.   (6 marks)

OCR A2 Economics

ⓔ Reference is made to macroeconomic policies and therefore is limited to fiscal, monetary, exchange rate and supply-side policies. There is no need to deal with policies on a small scale.

> **(c) Comment on the extent to which the policies you have identified may be successful in achieving their target.**   (10 marks)

ⓔ This question requires an evaluation of whether the policies have or have not worked. Full marks will not be achieved if only success or failure is explained.

ⓔ Reading the pre-issued materials will have concentrated your mind, but your answers do not require specific reference back to the case study. A diagram may help in part (a).

> **(2) (a) Why does poverty often occur in countries where agriculture is a large proportion of total output?**   (4 marks)

ⓔ This does not require reference to the materials but parts (b) and (c) do. Judge the amount of time required to answer each question by reference to the mark allocation.

> **(b) Analyse the theory of comparative advantage in relation to the Chinese economy.**   (6 marks)

ⓔ If you are going to use an example to illustrate, then make sure it identifies one country which has an absolute advantage in both products and different opportunity costs.

> **(c) Comment on the fact that Brazil is rich in natural resources but is still considered a less developed country.**   (10 marks)

ⓔ This involves a discussion about why some countries with natural resources have achieved a more developed status while others have been left behind. It is also possible to compare these countries with those that have achieved a higher status even though they have very few natural resources.

> **(3*) Discuss the extent to which less developed countries and more developed countries should adopt policies to protect their domestic industry.**   (20 marks)

ⓔ To achieve full marks in any 'discuss' question, you must identify two or more points of view, otherwise you are carrying out an explanation or analysis. A significant number of marks (approximately 8 marks) will be lost if you do not attempt a discussion. Also, this answer will allow up to 4 marks for the quality of written communication and must be written in continuous prose.

Mark scheme

(1) (a) As the question does not ask for an illustration, it is possible to achieve the full marks without using a diagram, but the better answers are likely to include a diagram of production possibility boundaries. Actual growth occurs when previously unemployed resources move the economy closer to a boundary, while potential economic growth shifts the boundary. Each definition will gain 1 mark, with the remaining 2 marks being given for highlighting points of distinction. (4 marks)

(b) The answer may refer to demand-side policies, such as fiscal, monetary and exchange rate policies, as ways in which actual growth can be promoted where

an economy has unemployed resources. Supply-side policies may be referred to as those which shift the production possibility boundary outwards. It is also possible to make reference to fiscal policy with supply-side intent, e.g. government expenditure on research and development, and monetary policy with supply-side intent as the effect of lower interest rates on investment. Either of these will promote potential economic growth. (6 marks)

(c) Again, it is likely that there will be a split between supply-side and demand-side policies. The issue with demand-side policies is the extent to which they can be successful in increasing the employment of unused factors. The answer may look at the different shapes for aggregate supply curves, where the horizontal shape gives scope to shift demand and raise output, while the long-run vertical aggregate supply curve does not respond to demand but requires a shift in the supply curve. It is also necessary to be critical of the supply-side policies such as research and development, investment, motivation etc. which may or may not be successful. In order to achieve the top range of marks, it is important to use evaluative comments and consider the extent to which countries have and have not been successful in utilising these policies. (10 marks)

(2) (a) Reference to extract 3 gives some hints of the problem where an economy is based mainly on agriculture. Output is variable and influenced by good and bad weather. Also supply and demand curves are relatively inelastic, which produces price volatility and income and job insecurity in the industry. A good year for crops is often a bad year for farm incomes and a bad year is good for those farmers who manage to produce reasonable amounts. To achieve full marks, four separate points of explanation or two well-explained points will be sufficient. (4 marks)

(b) Because this question asks you to analyse, it is useful to explain clearly, with an example, the theory of comparative advantage and then use extract 2 to identify the areas where China may have this comparative advantage. There will be 4 marks for a clear analysis of comparative advantage and 2 marks for setting it within the context of China. (6 marks)

(c) Given the information in extract 1, it is possible to identify the importance of agriculture in terms of coffee and as something that may well have held the country back, while the moves into steel production, arms manufacturing and car production may be moving it forward towards a more developed status. As with all countries, the institutions and infrastructure may not yet be in place to utilise the available resources fully. There is also mention of key economic problems such as spiralling inflation, massive long-term debt and corruption in the political system. Overall, the answer needs to be a balanced commentary on what has held back Brazil's development and what may be moving the country out of its less developed status. If no reference is made to Brazil, no more than 8 marks will be given. (10 marks)

(3) Extracts 4 and 5 give information about the USA using protectionist measures against China and can be used to build a case for protection. As it is a discussion, it is necessary to look at the case for and against protection. Points in favour of protection could include:
- protection of infant industry
- protection of senile industry regeneration
- protection against unfair trading practices, such as dumping, and from monopoly suppliers

- protection against illegal products, e.g. drugs
- maintaining national security
- employment protection
- providing a source of government revenue

Points against may include:
- not allowing the theory of comparative advantage to allocate resources efficiently
- potential for protection of inefficient industry to become permanent
- possibility that infant industries will never grow up
- retaliation from other countries
- raising of the cost of living
- restriction of consumer choice

The other point that the question addresses is whether it makes a difference if you are looking at less developed rather than more developed countries. The main points that need to be covered are the fact that you may be dealing with life and death problems in less developed countries and that these countries may need to protect themselves against large supranational organisations such as the EU (particularly the damage caused to them by the Common Agricultural Policy).

For a one-sided answer, the maximum marks that could be achieved will be 10, whereas a well-balanced evaluative discussion will achieve up to 16 marks with 4 marks allocated to the presentation and quality of the written communication. (20 marks)

A-grade answer

(1) (a)

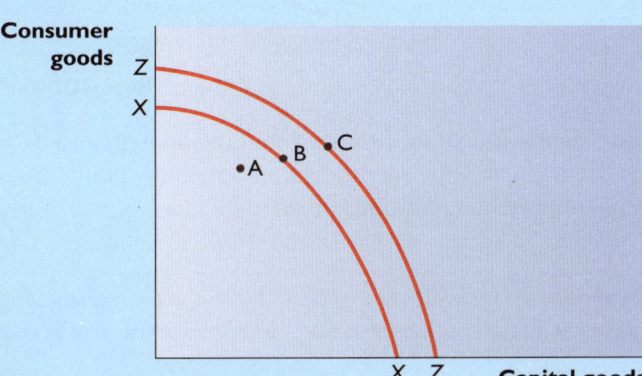

In an economy there may be unemployed resources and the country could be producing at point A in the diagram above. Actual growth will take place if those unemployed resources are put to work and the joint output of capital and consumer goods moves from A to B. If there is an increase in the productive capacity of the economy then potential economic growth is illustrated by a shift in the production possibility boundary as output moves from B to C.

ⓔ **4/4 marks awarded.** This answer contains a clear distinction between the two concepts of growth and makes good use of the diagram.

(b) Macroeconomic policies include monetary policy, which uses changes in the money supply and rate of interest to manage the overall level of aggregate demand; fiscal policy, which uses government budgets to manage aggregate demand; exchange rate policy, which changes the aggregate balance of demand between imports and exports; and a group of supply-side policies.

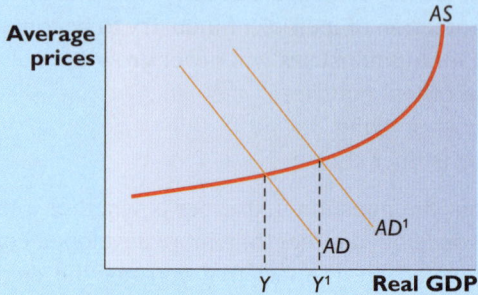

It is generally accepted that demand-side policies such as fiscal and monetary policy which shift aggregate demand from *AD* to *AD*[1] are best suited to raising actual output if it is below full employment output.

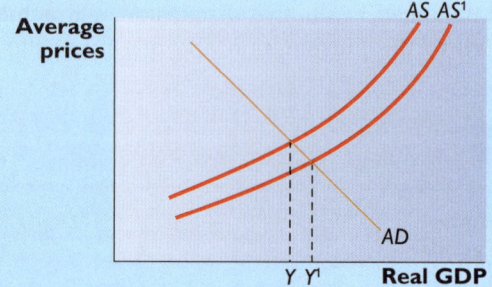

In contrast, supply-side policies which shift the aggregate supply curve from *AS* to *AS*[1] are going to shift the production possibility boundary outward and be a source of potential economic growth.

🄔 **5/6 marks awarded.** This answer gives a full but not complete identification of macroeconomic policies and how they can be used to promote actual growth and potential economic growth.

(c) There is considerable debate about whether demand management policies have any long-term effect on the economy, or even any short-term effect that is beneficial. For example, if the aggregate supply curve is vertical, then shifts in the aggregate demand curve caused by fiscal and monetary policy would just produce a rise or fall in the average level of prices, as illustrated below.

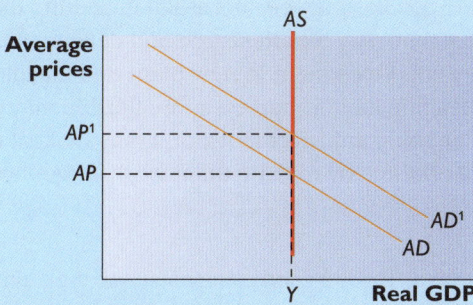

On the contrary, if the aggregate supply curve was horizontal, then shifts in aggregate demand would raise or lower real GDP without any effect on prices until the point of full employment is achieved, as illustrated below.

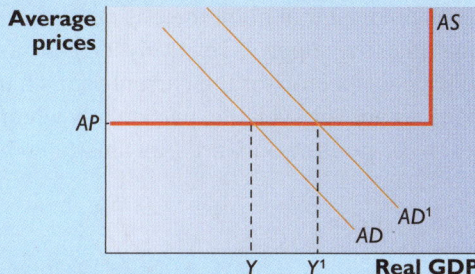

If there is a normal upward-sloping supply curve, then there will be a trade-off between inflation and changes in real GDP when aggregate demand shifts.

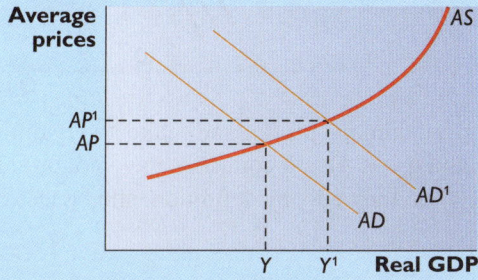

Exchange rate adjustments can bring about improvements in the balance of payments position, dependent upon the elasticities of demand for exports and imports. A currency depreciation (or devaluation, if the currency is fixed) will lower the prices of exports and raise the price of imports. This may help get rid of a balance of payments current account deficit. However, it may not help to solve the more deep-seated problem which caused the deficit, e.g. loss of competitiveness in UK industry or government mismanagement of the money supply.

Supply-side policies may be successful in shifting the aggregate supply curve to the right or they may not. Research and development may provide efficiency gains or may not. Investment in new plant and machinery may be effective or it may not. Making labour markets more flexible may produce one-off gains rather than ongoing improvements, or it may make it easier for employers to exploit the workforce by making them work longer hours for less pay.

ⓔ **8/10 marks awarded.** This is a good commentary on the main macroeconomic policies and whether they are successful in achieving some of their targets.

(2) (a) Many of the poorest countries in the world are locked into a cycle of subsistence, where agriculture provides almost all of their national output. The demand for farm produce is fairly inelastic. A certain amount of it is essential to life, but past that point there is no further demand for food.

At the same time, the supply is relatively inelastic as it is very difficult to increase the supply of a crop for the current year's harvest. The result is that agricultural prices are very volatile, particularly when a variable supply shifts the supply curve inwards or outwards, as illustrated below.

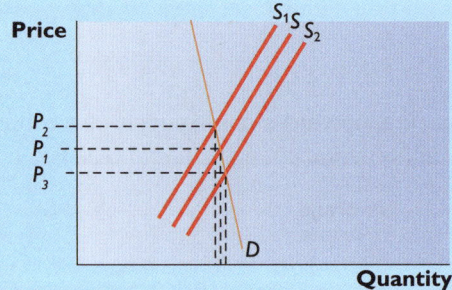

Volatile prices damage profits and make it very difficult for an economy to stabilise and grow. Also if countries have not produced much past subsistence, then they will, by definition, still be less developed.

ⓔ **4/4 marks awarded.** This is a good attempt at relating agricultural economies to poverty.

(b) It does not matter whether or not one country has absolute advantage over another country in the production of any one product, as long as it has a comparative advantage. In order for there to be gains from trade, a country must have lower opportunity costs of production. For example, if America and China could produce the following quantities of raw products given the same resources, then:

	Product X	Product Y
America	100 (3)	300 (1/3)
China	50 (5)	250 (1/5)

Opportunity costs in brackets

If America now specialises in product X and China in product Y, then both countries can gain from trade.

In extract 2 it is pointed out that China has 1.3 billion people, so it might be expected that it has a comparative advantage in the production of labour-intensive products. However, approximately 45% of its exports are in fact high end capital intensive products. This suggests that China has a comparative advantage over a wider range of products than was originally thought.

ⓔ **5/6 marks awarded.** This answer understands comparative advantage but could have gone a little further in the application of the theory.

(c) Many more developed countries have little access to natural resources, e.g. Japan, while less developed countries like Brazil are rich in resources but behind in the race for economic growth and development.

In extract 1 it is argued that there are a number of problems which have held back the latter's economic development. Firstly the political system has been accused of corruption and also holding back on infrastructure developments that are the essential framework from within which growth can take place. This factor also discourages foreign direct investment, as do the indicators of an unstable economy such as volatile inflation and rising unemployment. One other major problem is the exceptionally large government long-term debt. There are signs that Brazil is beginning to grow faster as it begins to develop its secondary and tertiary industries.

ⓔ **6/10 marks awarded.** Some good points are covered, but these could have been developed in more relevant detail.

(3) The arguments for and against more developed and less developed countries erecting protective barriers are very similar, although there are a few subtle differences that will be considered.

Concerns about a worldwide recession, possibly leading to a prolonged depression, encourage countries to look at protecting their domestic industries and maintaining jobs within their own economies. Even during the good times, a case can be made for protecting infant industries while they establish themselves and reduce their unit costs to a point where they can be competitive in a world market. This same argument can be applied to mature industries that have declined but could, if protected, regenerate themselves and once again become effective players. The American car industry is often described in this way. In fact, a lot of American industry is feeling threatened by the growth of giant companies in China that are threatening to cause job losses in textile and electronics manufacturing.

There is a sound economic argument for countries to protect themselves against unfair trading practices — the obvious example being where an industry is dumping its products at less than the cost of production in an attempt to destroy competition. Also a country may want to protect itself against products that

could be harmful to society, such as drugs. In the past, it has been argued that, for security reasons, a country needs to protect its agriculture even when it is inefficient; because an army marches on its stomach, no food means that, in a war, that country could not be successful if its food source was cut off. A less sound economic policy, but nevertheless relevant, is that protection in the form of tariffs does produce a useful source of revenue for the government that imposes them.

For less developed countries, the arguments used above are often even more critical as people may already be on or below the poverty line and unable to protect themselves. Also there are big supranational organisations like the EU and its Common Agricultural Policy which are damaging less developed countries; they need to protect themselves, as revenue from agriculture is a significant earner in home and foreign markets.

The main economic argument against protection is the theory of comparative advantage. This states that if all countries trade freely with each other and specialise in producing those products for which they have the lower opportunity cost, then there will be gains from trade and an efficient allocation of resources. Alternatively, protection raises the cost of living, reduces consumer choice and brings about a more inefficient allocation of resources. Recognition of this is why the World Trade Organization is trying to lower the current trade barriers between countries.

Evidence has shown that when one country raises a protective barrier against other countries, retaliation very soon removes any advantage and creates a further distortion to the free trade model. The result then tends to be a competitive raising of protective barriers and a greater inefficiency in resource allocation. The argument against protecting a mature industry while it regenerates is that it may never be able to stand alone as it has subsequently lost its comparative advantage. Also the infant industry may not have a comparative advantage or, under the banner of protection, it may never grow up. It is a very difficult political decision to remove protection as it can be seen to disadvantage the domestic economy and give advantage to foreign countries.

Although there are sound arguments for protection where there is not a level playing field for free competitive trade, it is generally felt by economists that less protection and more free trade will improve real GDP and living standards across the world.

🄴 **16/20 marks awarded.** This is a good evaluative discussion and well written, but it did not make as much use as it could have done of the extracts and did not mention much about the various forms of protection that exist. The mark allocation is 12 for content and 4 for the quality of written communication.

🄴 **Scored 48/60 = 80% = Grade A**

Paper 2 **extracts**

Extract 1 International debt

For many less developed countries (LDCs), initiating a process of economic development is impossible without some form of external help. Some have looked to foreign direct investment (FDI), some have relied on flows of overseas assistance, while others have tried to borrow on international financial markets to obtain the funds needed. However, for many countries (especially in sub-Saharan Africa), none of these sources has proved effective.

Table 1 shows data for a selection of LDCs at different levels of average income, ranging from Burundi (GDP per capita of just $106 in 2005) to Belize (GDP per capita of $3,786 in 2005). GDP per capita in US dollars may not give a picture of the real purchasing power of local income. For this reason, the table also shows GDP per capita measured in **purchasing power parity** dollars (PPP$). This measure is designed to be a better reflection of the real purchasing power of local income in different countries. If you run your eye down the columns, you will see that there is not a perfect correlation between the two measures.

The human development index (HDI), also shown in the table, provides a broader indicator of the level of human development achieved in each country. It is based on GDP per capita (in PPP$), adult literacy, school enrolment and life expectancy. This index varies between 0 and 1, with the higher values indicating a higher level of human development. The three components are intended to capture three aspects of development — namely, the resources available, knowledge to use those resources well and a reasonable lifespan in which to enjoy the consumption of those resources.

Overseas assistance is provided through a committee of the Organisation for Economic Cooperation and Development (OECD) and is known as **Overseas Development Assistance (ODA)**. Table 1 shows something of the importance of ODA from the perspective of the recipient countries. Notice Burundi, where almost half of GDP in 2005 was ODA. This suggests a high degree of dependence on such funding.

Back in 1974, the industrial nations of the world pledged that they would donate 0.7% of their GDP to providing ODA. This pledge was reiterated at the Millennium Summit in 2000. A handful of countries in northern Europe have reached the target, but for many other countries ODA has fallen well short.

Table 1 International debt, Overseas Development Assistance and less developed countries

	GDP per capita US$ 2005	GDP per capita PPP$ 2005	Human development index 2005	Net foreign direct investment inflows % of GDP		Overseas Development Assistance (ODA) % of GDP		Total debt service % of GDP		% of exports	
				1990	2005	1990	2005	1990	2005	1990	2005
Burundi	106	699	0.413	0.1	0.1	23.2	45.6	3.7	4.9	43.4	41.4
Ethiopia	157	1055	0.406	0.1	2.4	8.4	17.3	2.0	0.8	39.0	4.1
Rwanda	238	1206	0.452	0.3	0.4	11.1	26.7	0.8	1.1	14.2	8.1
Nepal	272	1550	0.534	0.2	0.0	11.7	5.8	1.9	1.6	15.7	4.6
Uganda	303	1454	0.505	-0.1	2.9	15.4	13.7	3.4	2.0	81.4	9.2
Gambia	304	1921	0.502	4.5	11.3	30.7	12.6	11.9	6.3	22.2	12.0
Tanzania	316	744	0.467	0.0	3.9	27.3	12.4	4.2	1.1	32.9	4.3
Mozambique	335	1242	0.384	0.4	1.6	40.5	19.4	3.2	1.4	26.2	4.2
Bangladesh	423	2053	0.547	0.0	1.3	6.9	2.2	2.5	1.3	25.8	5.3
Ghana	485	2480	0.553	0.3	1.0	9.5	10.4	6.2	2.7	38.1	7.1
Kenya	547	1240	0.521	0.7	0.1	13.8	4.1	9.2	1.3	35.4	4.4
Pakistan	711	2370	0.551	0.6	2.0	2.8	1.5	4.8	2.2	21.3	10.2
India	736	3452	0.619	0.1	0.8	0.4	0.2	2.6	3.0	31.9	19.1
Nigeria	752	1128	0.470	2.1	2.0	0.9	6.5	11.7	9.0	22.6	15.8
Sudan	760	2083	0.526	-0.2	8.4	6.2	6.6	0.4	1.4	8.7	6.5
Côte d'Ivoire	900	1648	0.432	0.4	1.6	6.4	0.7	11.7	2.8	35.4	5.5
Bolivia	1017	2819	0.695	0.6	-3.0	11.2	6.2	7.9	5.7	38.6	14.8
Philippines	1192	5137	0.771	1.2	1.1	2.9	0.6	8.1	10.0	27.0	16.7
Indonesia	1302	3843	0.728	1.0	1.8	1.5	0.9	8.7	6.3	33.3	22.0
China	1713	6757	0.777	1.0	3.5	0.6	0.1	2.0	1.2	11.7	3.1
Peru	2838	6039	0.773	0.2	3.2	1.5	0.5	1.8	7.0	10.8	26.0
Belize	3786	7109	0.778	4.2	11.4	7.3	1.2	4.4	20.7	6.8	34.5

Source: HDR 2007/2008.

Note: the countries are in ascending order of GDP per capita in US$.

Extract 2   African exports and globalisation

One important facet of globalisation is the increase in global trade flows. The primary purpose of the World Trade Organization (WTO), which was established in 1995, is to bring member countries together to negotiate reductions in barriers and distortions to trade. One effect of this should be to increase volumes of trade. Between 1948 and 1999, global trade flows increased on average by 8% per annum, a 16-fold increase over the half century. For developing countries as a group, exports and imports were each equivalent to about 15% of GDP in 1975 but both had doubled to more than 30% of GDP by 2008. As markets become more integrated and as firms become increasingly international (even if not multinationals, they may subcontract or outsource globally), one expects trade to increase. At a global level this has been the case, but it is not true of all regions.

Africa, in particular, has not shared in the global increase in trade flows. The African region accounted for just over 3% of world merchandise exports in 1990, but this declined to a 2.3% share in 2000. Over the same period, Africa's share of world merchandise imports also fell. The dollar value (in current terms) of exports from Africa actually declined in the 1980s and rose by only 3% in the 1990s. The value of imports, in contrast, has been quite stable. Why is this the case? This article considers two factors in the explanation: the types of products Africa exports and restrictive trade policies.

African exports

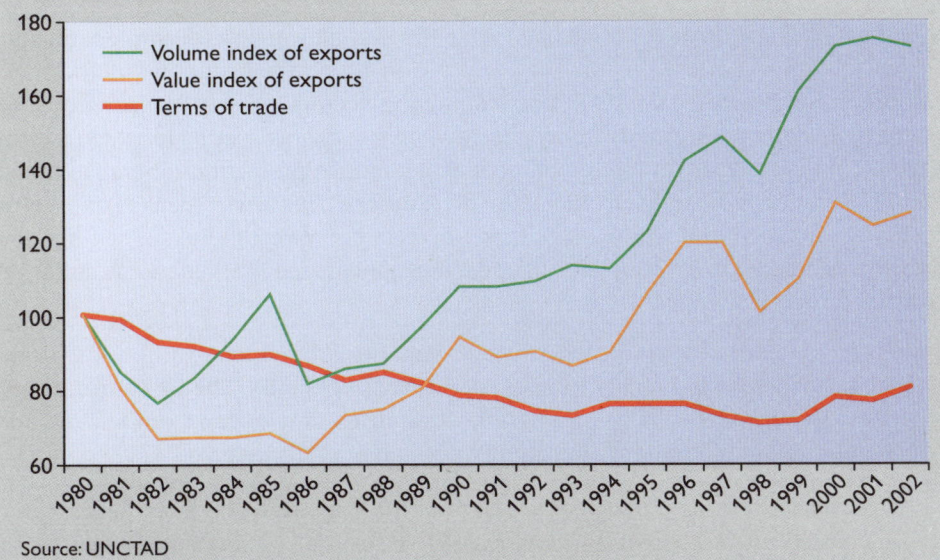

Source: UNCTAD

Figure 1 Volume and value index of exports of sub-Saharan Africa and terms of trade, 1980–2002 (1980 = 100)

The first factor is illustrated in Figure 1. Between 1980 and 2002, the volume (or quantity) of sub-Saharan African (SSA) exports rose by some 70% fairly steadily over the period. The SSA countries were exporting more. However, the value of these exports only increased by 20% — and actually declined in the 1980s — and was quite volatile from year to year. This is because SSA countries export mostly

primary commodities, the prices of which are determined on world markets and are volatile. One can also see that SSA's terms of trade, the relative prices of imports and exports (the quantity of imports that can be purchased by a unit of exports) also declined by about 20%, and this decline was quite steady. In other words, although the quantity of exports was increased, their value was falling in dollar terms and in purchasing power (for imports).

An important part of the explanation for the poor export performance of SSA is that the prices of the products exported by SSA — mostly primary commodities — were declining relative to the prices of products exported by other countries (and imported by SSA), especially manufactures. One implication is that, even if SSA countries liberalised their trade policies, the impact on the value of exports might be quite limited. This article examines this issue, looking at the African experience over the past two decades. First, it is important to consider the arguments for trade liberalisation.

Why trade policy reform?

Economists disagree about many things, but one proposition that attracts widespread agreement is that high trade barriers damage the economy. If a country imposes high tariffs or other restrictions on imports to protect domestic producers, this benefits producers of import-competing goods (who can charge higher prices and earn economic rents) but is a disincentive to producers of exports, who are not protected and face higher prices for inputs.

Note that, because other countries' access to the market is restricted, protection also harms foreign exporters. In this way, protection promotes economic inefficiency: resources are directed towards import-competing sectors, where the economy may not have any comparative advantage, and away from export sectors in which it does have a comparative advantage. When countries reduce protection (liberalise trade) they encourage a more efficient allocation of resources. This is why the WTO promotes trade liberalisation and why it is multilateral. If all countries liberalise together, the potential benefits are greater, such as those from increased market access and from reduced protection.

There are four broad ways in which trade benefits an economy, and reforms are intended to increase the ability to make use of these benefits. The first three, taken together, are the static gains from trade. Countries can expand production and consumption possibilities and allocate resources more efficiently.

1   Trade implies that the country has access to a global market that is much larger than the domestic market. For many items, production costs fall as the volume produced increases, so access to a larger market increases the amount that can be produced competitively. This is especially beneficial for small countries.

2   Trade encourages a more efficient allocation of resources. Countries are encouraged to concentrate on producing goods in which they are internationally competitive. These are then exchanged globally for goods the country cannot produce efficiently (exports are traded for imports).

3 Imports increase consumption possibilities by expanding the variety of goods available. A country can gain access to goods it is unable to produce itself, or at least that it is unable to produce efficiently.

4 Trade can contribute to economic growth, generating long-run gains. As countries engage in trade, they engage with the rest of the world. There are incentives to take advantage of new techniques and technologies in order to increase efficiency. Increases in efficiency and trade stimulate growth. There is also a macroeconomic stimulation to growth as exports earn foreign exchange. Imported inputs and technology can be purchased with this, thereby permitting domestic demand to grow faster without generating a balance of payments deficit.

Extract 3 Development profile: Country F

In terms of GDP per capita (at US$240 in 2003), Country F is among the poorest countries in the world, although it falls within the UNDP's medium range in terms of the human development index. Its population was just below 25 million in 2003. Geographically, Country F is mountainous and landlocked. Only 20% of the total land area is cultivable, although it is estimated that about three-quarters of the population depend upon agriculture for their livelihoods.

The country has high potential for developing tourism, but this has been hampered in recent years by political upheaval and civil conflict. The country became a multiparty democracy only in 1990, but the role of the monarchy continued to be a strong influence on its governance. In 2001, the heir to the throne's choice of wife was rejected by his parents, reportedly triggering a killing spree that left him and his parents dead. His uncle inherited the throne. A group of rebels launched an insurgency that has claimed 11,000 lives in the early part of the twenty-first century. In February 2005, the king dismissed the government and assumed full executive powers in the name of combating the insurgency. This intensified the conflict and in April 2006 (under foreign pressure), the king announced that power would be returned to the people. Parliament has now been reassembled and a ceasefire agreed with the rebels.

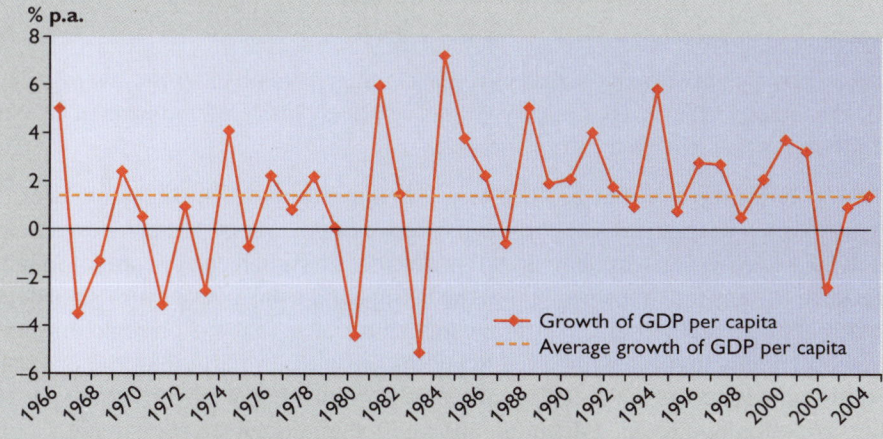

Figure 1 Country F: growth of GDP per capita

Figure 1 shows the growth path of GDP per capita since 1966. The spiky appearance of the graph indicates that growth fluctuated quite a bit from one year to the next. The negative growth shown in 2002 probably reflects the political turmoil of the period. Although the growth rate then seems to have returned to the average (1.33%), this average is still low. In spite of the political unrest, Figure 2 shows a steady improvement in the level of human development since 1975.

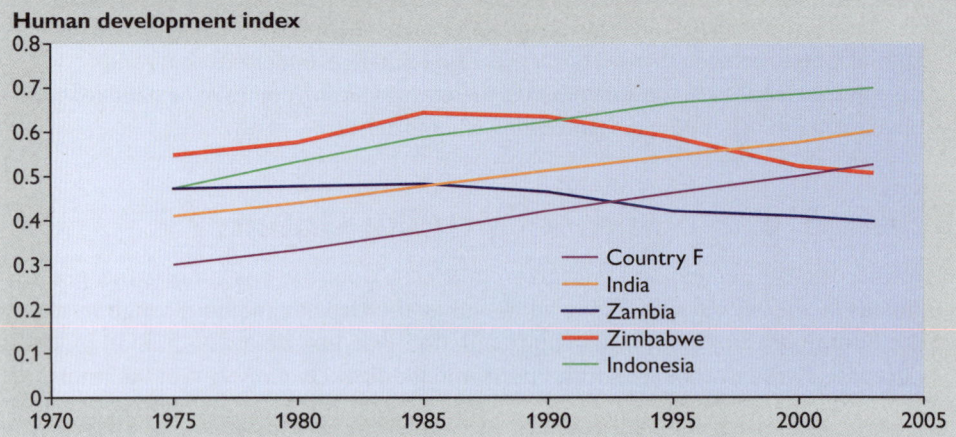

Figure 2 Trends in the human development index

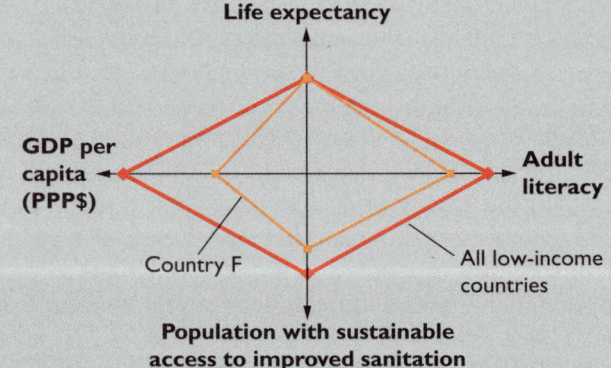

Figure 3 Development diamond comparing Country F with all low-income countries

Figure 3 shows a development diamond for Country F relative to the average level for all low-income countries. Country F fares relatively less well in terms of GDP per capita than for the other indicators shown.

The World Bank reports that the Country F Living Standards Survey conducted in 2003/04 found a dramatic decline in the incidence of poverty by 11 percentage points since 1995/96. However, it appears that this decline is as much due to conflict-induced migration as to any real improvement in the living conditions of Country F's residents. The World Bank's recommended strategy for Country F is to focus on removing some of the bottlenecks that have impeded economic growth; in particular, the excessive role of the state and the lack of adequate infrastructure, especially in terms of water supply, irrigation and roads. Education and healthcare also need investment.

Data used in this profile were taken from the *Human Development Report 2005* and *World Development Report 2006*.

Extract 4   The WTO and the Doha declaration

In December 2005, the World Trade Organization (WTO) holds its ministerial conference in Hong Kong — a meeting which could have a major influence on the future of international trade. Here we look at some of the economic issues that are at stake.

The WTO

For most of the period since the Second World War, the conduct of international trade has been directed by the General Agreement on Tariffs and Trade (GATT), which was responsible for organising a series of rounds of tariff reductions. The last round under the GATT was the Uruguay round, completed in 1994.

Dispute settlement

After the completion of the Uruguay round, the WTO was formed. The WTO's function was to continue to encourage tariff reductions but also to take a role in providing a framework for the settlement of trade disputes between countries, especially in terms of persuading countries to become less protectionist in attitude. In the first 8 years of its life, the WTO received 300 cases to investigate — about the same number dealt with in the entire life of the GATT from 1947 to 1994.

An important part of the WTO's brief was to expand the remit of trade discussions to include agriculture and services, which had been considered too contentious for the GATT. Negotiations on these key topics began in early 2000 but progress has been slow — perhaps not surprising, given the measures in force to protect agriculture in economies such as the USA and the European Union.

Other disputes have at times threatened progress. For example, there has been an ongoing dispute between the USA and Europe over subsidies provided to their respective aircraft manufacturers, Boeing and Airbus. The USA has complained that Airbus has had unfair subsidies from the EU and the EU has countered by claiming that Boeing has also received indirect subsidies from the US government.

This is an industry complicated by the military spin-offs of aeronautical research, which makes it difficult to disentangle the commercial and military research and development expenses. However, it can be argued that the net result has been favourable for consumers, as the two companies have competed intensely with each other, whereas had Airbus not received help, Boeing would probably have been unchallenged as a global monopoly in the industry.

After the Uruguay round

After the last completed round of trade negotiations in Uruguay in 1994, the newly-established WTO began negotiations for the next round. The first ministerial conference was in Seattle in 1999, but this made little progress and was seriously disrupted by at least 30,000 anti-globalisation protesters who mounted major demonstrations. It was in Doha (Qatar) that the round was finally launched and given the name of that city, in a long-established tradition. The meeting took place in

November 2001, with the aim of creating a set of trading arrangements that would be fairer to developing countries.

Indeed, the Doha conference went even further by setting out the Doha Development Agenda, attempting to highlight the importance of establishing conditions for international trade that would encourage trade with less developed countries and thus enable them to develop more rapidly.

Cancún

In September 2003, a further summit was held in Cancún, Mexico, to assess progress towards the Doha agenda and to move things forward in four main areas: agriculture, industrial goods, trade in services and a new customs code.

However, those talks failed. A new alliance of developing countries emerged that refused to sign a proposed agreement which they felt favoured the richer WTO members. The main sticking point was on agriculture. This is especially important for many developing countries, whose economies remain heavily reliant on agriculture for employment and income.

A key target of criticism of the more developed countries was the extensive subsidies provided to agriculture. For example, in 2004, the EU spent around half of its entire budget on various measures to support its farmers, although farmers comprise only about 3% of the EU's population.

After Cancún, there seemed a strong possibility that the Doha agenda would be abandoned completely. However, during the following months, the WTO continued to chip away at various protectionist measures, for example declaring that US duties on imported steel and subsidies to cotton farmers were illegal.

Geneva

Members of the WTO came together at another summit meeting in Geneva in 2004 and finally it seemed that some progress was being made. Agreement was reached with key nations (including the USA, the EU, Brazil and Japan) to start eliminating export subsidies and lowering tariff barriers. In particular, agreement was reached on reducing subsidies on sugar within the EU — this having been an important area of contention. In return, developing countries agreed to cut tariffs on manufactured goods.

Paris

Ministers from 30 WTO member nations met in Paris in May 2005 to consider proposals from the EU on reforming the tariff structure for agricultural imports. The proposal was that tariffs should be converted into a percentage of a good's price, rather than a flat rate of euros per tonne. This may seem a technicality, but many regarded it as a significant concession by the EU.

Hong Kong

All this sets the scene for the key meeting of the WTO members in Hong Kong in December 2005. International trade is crucial for all countries and the terms under which trade takes place are also critical, as these terms determine which countries gain the most from engaging in international trade. For many years some economists have been arguing that less developed countries will not be able to embark on a process of economic development until the more developed countries are prepared to cooperate. There are still some European countries deeply committed to maintaining support for agriculture, especially France, for whom the sector holds especial significance.

However, it is to be hoped that the Hong Kong meetings about the Doha Development Agenda will see some progress being made in establishing a framework for international trade, in which all countries can feel they have been fairly treated.

Director-General Pascal Lamy, in his 2012 report, says that the future of Doha is 'to move forward in small steps'.

Extract 5 Economic growth in developing countries

The adequacy of savings

A first difficulty arises if the developing country is unable to generate a flow of savings. In many countries where average incomes are low, it is difficult to encourage voluntary savings by households, especially when a high proportion of the population is located in rural areas and dependent on agriculture. Furthermore, local firms may not generate a sufficient surplus in order to provide a flow of funds for investment.

In such a situation, the question arises as to whether the government is able to take action to overcome the difficulty of mobilising savings and funds for investment. Given that it may not be easy to raise revenue through taxation when the tax base is small and tax collection difficult, the government may be tempted to raise funds through printing money. However, this could be counter-productive, as it is likely to lead to higher inflation.

Investment and productive capacity

The difficulties do not stop there. Even if a developing country could raise the funds needed for investment, there are many competing demands for the use of those funds, not all of which may lead directly to economic growth. For example, it may be that there is a need for infrastructure investment to provide facilities such as housing, sanitation or water supply. It may be that there is a need to invest in various forms of human capital — improved nutrition, healthcare or education. Such investment may be vital for the alleviation of poverty and for improving living conditions, but may not

lead directly to economic growth, although we would expect there to be indirect (and probably long-term) effects.

It is also important to realise that there may be many reasons why investment will not be carried out effectively in some developing countries. For example, where there is a lack of entrepreneurial talent, it may not be possible to identify the best investment opportunities. Where there is weak governance, it may be that funds are channelled into unproductive routes, or even appropriated by corrupt officials.

Income and savings

If, in spite of all these obstacles, we do witness an improvement in the rate of economic growth, is there any guarantee that increased income will feed back into savings? Not necessarily. It could be that funds will be used for consumption rather than for savings — and this is especially likely in a country where average incomes are low.

Mobilising savings

Even if it were possible to generate a flow of savings, it is then crucial to be able to make use of those savings for productive investment. This requires the existence and effectiveness of financial institutions, such as savings banks. Here again, many developing countries face difficulties, as their financial institutions also tend to be under-developed. Indeed, for many people living in rural areas, there may be no access to formal financial institutions — or little confidence to encourage people to deposit their savings in them.

It has been well documented that in many developing countries, people tend to save by purchasing fixed assets. This could be in the form of additional plots of land lying fallow, physical assets such as a bicycle or gold, or perhaps an extra chicken or two. Some people hoard their savings as cash under the bed. These forms of savings do not contribute to economic growth, as they cannot be converted into funds which a potential investor could borrow in order to undertake investment.

Paper 2 questions

Time allowed: 2 hours

A clean copy of the pre-issued stimulus material is included with the question paper. Answer all the questions. You will be assessed on the quality of written communication in question 3.

Total marks allocated: 60

(1) (a) Distinguish between economic growth and economic development. (4 marks)

 To achieve the full marks it is necessary to use comparative language and not just explain one, explain the other and leave the examiner to make the link.

(b) Analyse the GDP per capita and the HDI measures of economic development. (6 marks)

ⓔ Remember that GDP per capita is one of the constituents of the human development index.

(c) Examine the extent to which economic development can take place without economic growth. (10 marks)

ⓔ Because the question says 'Examine the extent', you must investigate whether economic development can take place without economic growth, as well as the obvious.

(2) (a) Is the exchange rate or the purchasing power parity a better comparative measure of countries' living standards? (4 marks)

ⓔ If you use a diagram to illustrate exchange rate determination, remember that you can only measure the price of one currency using another currency. Therefore if you are measuring the price of sterling, you will need the dollar or euro on the vertical axis. Also remember that it is demand which determines both the demand and supply curve for a currency, i.e. demand for exports determines the demand and demand for imports the supply.

(b) Identify the terms of trade and explain what is meant by a favourable and an unfavourable movement in the terms of trade. (6 marks)

ⓔ A common mistake is to confuse the terms of trade and the balance of trade. The terms of trade is only a price ratio while the balance of trade is a difference between two totals, i.e. imports and exports.

(c) Comment on the extent to which changes in the terms of trade identified in extract 2 can benefit the balance of payments of sub-Saharan economies. (10 marks)

ⓔ Because the question relates to an extract, it is important to make reference to it and describe how the unfavourable movement could have beneficial effects, as could the favourable movement.

(3*) Discuss the extent to which political stability is important in bringing about economic growth and development. (20 marks)

ⓔ The best way to approach this is to look at political stability as providing the level playing field on which the economy can grow. The type of political stability may vary between countries, as China offers political stability without democracy while other countries seem to function best within a democratic framework. As this is to be written in continuous prose, it is best to use an essay style, which is an introductory paragraph followed by a discussion and then a conclusion. As it is a discussion, look for examples of where the concepts go together and where one is not dependent on the others.

Mark scheme

(1) (a) The main point of distinction is that economic growth is a fairly narrow concept concerned with an increase in the per capita productive capacity of an economy. This could occur as the result of a reduction in the cost of producing armaments.

Economic development usually involves an increase in real per capita income, but it is more concerned with rising living standards through improving education, health, infrastructure etc. To achieve 4 marks, comparative statements must be made. (4 marks)

(b) Measuring GDP per capita in real terms (adjusted for inflation/deflation) will show an average change relative to population size and therefore be a useful indication of whether an economy is growing and developing. The human development index covers a wider range of issues which focus more clearly on people and address not only GDP per capita but also issues of education, health and life expectancy. The 6 marks are available for an analysis of both measures and a clear reference to their relevance to economic development. (6 marks)

(c) An examination of an issue requires a depth of investigation into how much economic development results from economic growth. You would be expected to provide an explanation of how economic growth can produce the additional resources that can be directed towards projects and can help develop the economy. However, to gain the full range of marks, it is necessary to examine also how economic development can take place without economic growth. Redistributive policies can explain this: for example a reduction in the production of non-productive capital (e.g. arms) and an increase in productive capital (e.g. factories). A simple redistribution of income where money is taken away from high-income earners produces greater benefit at the bottom end than is lost at the top end. A possible conclusion could point out that economic development, i.e. in the form of education, can produce economic growth. Without an examination of different points of view, marks would be limited to 6 out of 10. (10 marks)

(2) (a) The exchange rate is easily available and is a relatively crude measure which can identify differences between countries. The purchasing power parity, however, is a better measure of standards of living because it compares currencies by how much can be bought in each country and establishes a rate which more often than not is different from the exchange rate. (4 marks)

(b) In real terms, the terms of trade is how much of one product it is necessary to sell abroad in order to buy a foreign product. It is calculated using the formula:

$$\frac{\text{index number showing the average price of exports}}{\text{index number showing the average price of imports}} \times 100$$

There are 3 marks for the above, and the remaining 3 marks are awarded for saying that a favourable movement means a rise in the price of exports relative to imports, so that less exports need to be sold to buy the same quantity of imports, and vice versa for an unfavourable movement. (6 marks)

(c) The steady fall in the terms of trade between 1980 and 1998 would be considered an unfavourable movement, while the rise between 1998 and 2002 would be favourable.

Using elasticity and shifts in demand and supply curves, it is necessary to explain how favourable movements in the terms of trade can have favourable effects on the current account of the balance of payments. This will happen if the demand for exports and/or imports is inelastic. However, if demand is elastic, the effect will be opposite, i.e. a favourable movement in the terms of trade will have an unfavourable effect on the current balance of the external account.

The 10 marks will be allocated if the student shows a clear understanding of both effects. (10 marks)

(3) It is necessary to look at all the factors affecting economic growth and development, e.g.
- invention and innovation
- improvements in quality of labour
- investment in capital stock
- increased mobility of productive factors
- more efficient allocation of resources
- economies of scale
- motivation and the profit motive

In addition, or alternatively, the approach may be through the models of economic development:
- Rostow's model
- Harrod–Domar model
- Lewis–Fei–Ranis model
- dependency theories
- balanced and unbalanced growth theories

It is then important to look at whether the situations described above will work irrespective of the type and stability of a political environment, or whether it is necessary to have a certain political environment before the above can produce an increase in productive capacity per capita and the characteristics of development can flourish.

A full discussion will be marked out of 16, with 4 further marks awarded for quality of written communication. (20 marks)

A-grade answer

(1) **(a)** Economic growth takes place when there is an increase in productive capacity per person. It is illustrated by a shift in the production possibility frontier such that, with the same number of resources, more can be produced: AA to BB in the diagram below.

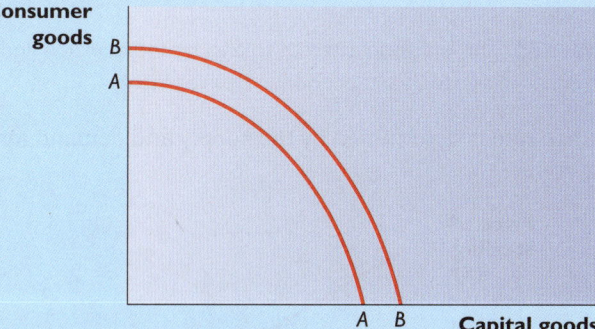

In contrast, economic development is a much broader concept as it specifies developments in education, health and the infrastructure of the economy.

🄔 **4/4 marks awarded.** This answer clearly shows an understanding of the narrow concept of economic growth and the broader concept of economic development.

(b) Gross domestic product is a measure of the total output of an economy over a specific period of time. It can increase as the result of actual growth, when a country uses more of its unemployed resource, or economic growth, when it increases its productive capacity per capita. Arguably an economy can show an increase in economic growth without showing an increase in the characteristics that are recognised as economic development. Economic development is generally concerned with sustainable improvements in living standards. In 1990 the United Nations introduced the human development index, which not only measures the growth in GDP but also uses a measure of life expectancy and education to illustrate that the economy is developing.

ⓔ 5/6 marks awarded. The answer shows an understanding of each concept and relates them to economic development.

(c) Economic growth means that more goods and services can be made available to the people in a country. Also more funds can be made available to government. This means that these additional resources could be used to promote education, improve health, develop the transportation and communication infrastructure. The provision of more and better public goods and public services can also take place.

In order to answer the question, it is necessary to decide whether the factors that are described as measures of economic development could come about without an increase in productive capacity per capita. Firstly, it is possible that actual output could grow as the result of using unemployed resources. In the past, deficit budgeting has been used directly to employ unemployed resources and promote development in the areas described above.

A further question to ask is whether this development can take place with no economic growth or actual growth. The answer is yes, if there is a redistribution of resources away from the production of goods and services that are not associated with economic development (warfare products) towards those products that are characteristic of economic development.

ⓔ 8/10 marks awarded. This is a good attempt to answer the question and untangle the relationship between economic growth and economic development.

(2) (a) The exchange rate is determined by the supply and demand for a currency, as illustrated below:

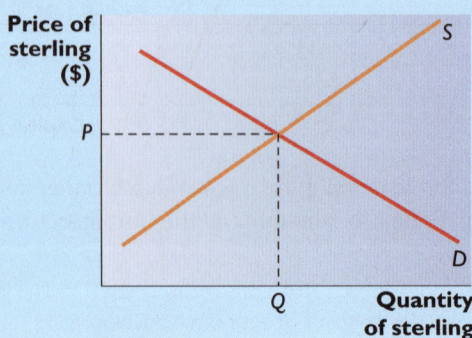

While the supply and demand for a currency is determined by the demand for imports and exports, one way to compare the income per head between two countries with different currencies is to use the exchange rate. However, it is not as precise as a comparison using purchasing power parity, which produces a currency valuation based upon the amount of currency required in each country to buy the same basket of products.

ⓔ **4/4 marks awarded.** The answer includes a clear statement that ppp is a better measure.

(b) The terms of trade are calculated using the following formula:

$$\text{terms of trade} = \frac{\text{index number for the average price of exports}}{\text{index number for the average price of imports}} \times 100$$

A movement is favourable when the terms of trade rise and unfavourable when they fall. What will make the terms of trade rise is an increase in export prices relative to import prices or a decrease in export prices which is not as steep as the decrease in import prices. Either means that the same amount of exports by value can now purchase more imports. For an unfavourable movement, the result would be that the same amount of exports by value will buy fewer imports.

ⓔ **5/6 marks awarded.** This shows a clear understanding of the terms of trade, although there was no mention of the real terms of trade.

(c) In extract 2 the terms of trade for sub-Saharan Africa fell from a base number of 100 in 1980 to a low of approximately 72 in 1998 and then rose again to just above 80 in 2000. Initially, there was a dip in the volume and value index for exports between 1980 and 1982, but then the value index rose between 1982 and 1986, even though there was a fall in the volume index. Despite some early volatility, which is common in primary product sales, the volume and value index of exports rose steadily as the terms of trade declined up until 1997. This is likely to be the result of a steady fall in the terms of trade, which would have made export prices relatively cheaper than import prices.

After a dip in the volume and value of exports in 1997/1998, both value and volume indices for exports rose, as well as the terms of trade. This means that export prices would have been rising relative to import prices and at the same time the sales and revenue from exports were rising. This is probably not the result of the elasticity of demand for exports, but more likely to be the result of the demand curve for exports shifting to the right as the world's demand for primary products was growing fast and countries like China and India were expanding rapidly.

ⓔ **8/10 marks awarded.** This is a good attempt at using the statistics, and some effort has been made to identify the extent to which terms of trade changes have benefited export sales.

(3) Many factors are involved in bringing about economic growth and development and these may vary from country to country in terms of their impact and importance.

Over many years, and usually centred on one country, inventions have produced an increase in economic growth rates that tend to spread out from the source. A map of the distribution of significant inventions has tended to show that more of them occur in capitalist economies where there is motivation and reward. The command economies that did not have a profit or reward motive have not figured high in the league table of inventions. So in this case, the political system may have played a part. Along with the inventions must go the innovations, and it is the role of the entrepreneur to see whether an invention is economically viable and can satisfy customer demand at a level which can make a profit. Political stability is important here, as the entrepreneur is taking a risk and political uncertainty is one of the things that will discourage innovation. Also multinational corporations that target new countries to develop their new ideas will tend to be attracted to countries that have a history of political stability. The result is that Singapore will tend to attract foreign direct investment whereas Zimbabwe will not.

In all countries that have grown and developed, there has been a considerable increase in the stock of capital per capita. It is therefore reasonable to assume that growth and development require a significant investment in new plant and machinery, factories and infrastructure. Bearing in mind that this will require access to savings which can be mobilised through a sound financial system and also direct investment by government, particularly in the infrastructure, then political stability is again important. In an unstable political situation, it will be difficult to raise taxes and to borrow the funds required to bring about this essential investment.

Running alongside investment in physical capital is investment in human capital. Education and training are considered particularly important in the less developed countries and the attitude of politicians to education can have a significant effect on improvements in human capital and therefore growth and development.

Underlying all these factors that may affect economic growth and development from within a country is the argument that trade is the real engine of growth: international trade allows economies of scale to be achieved and ideas to be shared around the world. At present there are many restrictions and the economists' argument is that, in order to benefit from the theory of comparative advantage, there must be no restraints on trade. Political instability is a restraint on trade as this may restrict imports or exports. The World Trade Organization is very concerned with reducing trade barriers and the Doha declaration, which came out of a meeting in Qatar in 2001, aimed at creating trade arrangements that would not disadvantage less developed countries.

It is clear from historical evidence that political stability is an important pre-requisite of economic growth and development. In itself, it will not bring about these required benefits, but without it growth and development will not take place at a significant rate and, as the instability gets worse, so there may be a total reversal to negative growth and a contraction in the human development index. Those countries that suffer internal strife, such as Zimbabwe and Iraq, are testament to this point of view.

e **17/20 marks awarded.** The answer shows a good understanding of some of the factors that are important in bringing about economic growth and development, and attempts a discussion about the extent to which political stability is important. Mark allocation is 13 for content and 4 for the quality of written communication.

e **Scored 51/60 = 85% = Grade A**

Paper 3 **extracts**

Extract 1	'The business cycle', Peter Smith, *OCR Advanced Economics*, pp. 142–43, Philip Allan Updates, 2006
Extracts 2 and 3	'Institutions and economic development', Jian Tong, *Economic Review*, Vol. 25, No. 3
Extract 4	Extracts from 'Economic growth in developing countries', Peter Smith, *Economic Review*, Vol. 23, No. 1
Extract 5	'Economic development and the environment', Graham Mallard, *Economic Review*, Vol. 24, No. 1

Extract 1 **The business cycle**

In the past it has not been uncommon for economies to go through a regular business cycle, where the level of economic activity has varied around an underlying trend. Figure 1 shows an economy in which real GDP is trending upwards over time but fluctuating around the trend, so that actual GDP follows a regular cycle around the trend. The point of maximum growth is often referred to as the *peak* of the cycle — or a *boom* period — whereas the low point is known as the *trough* of the cycle. If the growth rate is negative for two consecutive quarters, the economy is considered to be in *recession*.

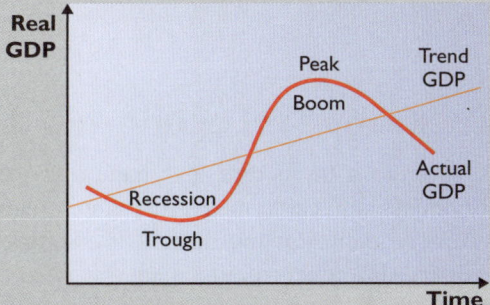

Figure 1 The business cycle

Figure 2 illustrates this in a different way, by showing the growth rates of real GDP in the UK over a cycle from 1984 to 1994.

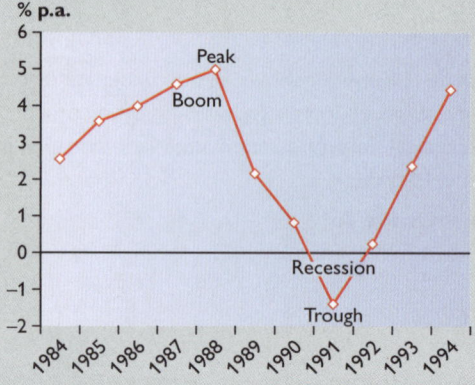

Source: Economic Trends Annual Supplement

Figure 2 Profile of a cycle: growth of real GDP, 1984–94 (% change over previous year)

A number of explanations have been advanced to explain the business cycle. One suggestion is that some governments engineer the cycle, taking the economy into a boom in the lead-up to an election, only to slow it down again once elected. This has become known as the *political business cycle*. Another suggestion is that cycles arise because of the lagged impact of policy measures on the economy: in other words, it takes time for policies to take effect — sometimes so long that they can destabilise the economy by having unintended effects.

In the past, considerable effort has gone into trying to predict the turning points of the business cycle by looking for *leading indicators* that turn in advance of the cycle — for example, the CBI quarterly survey of business optimism, which is designed to gather firms' views about the cycle. Changes in the number of new dwellings started and changes in consumer borrowing are also seen as leading indicators. In contrast, *coincident indicators* move in step with the current state of the business cycle — for example, real GDP or the volume of retail sales. On the other hand, unemployment tends to be a *lagging indicator*, as firms may not reduce their labour force right at the start of a recession, preferring first to ensure that it is not a temporary blip.

Extract 2 Institutions and economic development

There are enormous variations in income per capita across countries and an important task for economists is to explain why this is so. Understanding the causes of such inequality is a prerequisite for the design of effective policies to help the poorest nations. The current differences in income per capita between countries are a reflection of past variations in long-run economic growth rates, and this article examines the fundamental causes of growth.

Why study institutions?

One source of growth is the accumulation of physical capital. The more capital that individuals have to work with, the higher labour productivity, and hence income per capita, will be. However, it has been shown that the accumulation of physical capital alone cannot generate sustainable long-run growth. The reason is that, for a given level of technology, physical capital is subject to diminishing returns, i.e. the marginal product of capital is decreasing. The consequence is that, unless the diminishing returns to physical capital accumulation are offset by technological progress, the growth of per capita income will decline and eventually stop.

A second source of growth is the accumulation of human capital. The human capital stock of an economy consists of the knowledge and skills possessed by its labour force. It can be raised by investing in education and on-the-job training. By increasing the stock of human capital, these investments raise the level of labour productivity and hence per capita output. The importance of the accumulation of human capital is that it partially offsets the effect of diminishing returns to physical capital and thus helps sustain the growth of per capita income. However, it cannot fully compensate for diminishing returns to physical capital because the accumulation of human capital itself is subject to diminishing returns.

The implication is that a third factor, namely technological progress, is necessary for sustained growth. Technical progress, in turn, depends upon investments in research and development.

Economic growth cannot be taken for granted. The necessary investments in physical and human capital and in research and development typically involve market exchanges, and such exchanges are dependent on an institutional environment in which contracts are enforced and property rights protected. Consider, for example, a farmer who wants to borrow some money to invest in a land irrigation system. This would involve a contract (usually, but not necessarily, in written form) between the farmer and the lender. An important aspect of the situation is that borrowing and repayment necessarily occur at different times. This can leave the lender vulnerable to the borrower reneging on his/her part of the contract and since this problem can be anticipated by the prospective lender, the exchange may not occur in the first place.

Thus an institutional structure that serves to enforce contracts (for example, a legal system that provides penalties if parties do not honour contracts) is conducive to market exchange. This example also highlights the importance of secure property rights. A farmer who fears that his land might be appropriated by another party sometime in the future will be reluctant to incur the investment expense. The situation in Zimbabwe in recent years illustrates this point.

Extract 3 Institutions and economic development

Why have so many countries failed to adopt 'good' institutions?

Given this evidence, it is natural to ask why all countries do not adopt an institutional structure conducive to growth. Some countries have done so. Institutional innovations diffused from Britain to a number of other, mainly western, countries and indeed, the per capita income levels of these industrialised countries appear to have converged. Why, then, have the institutional innovations not spread from industrialised countries to less developed countries and so closed the gap of per capita income levels between rich and poor nations?

To answer this question, first we need to consider the nature of institutions in a little more detail. An institution can be defined as a system of rules, beliefs, norms and organisations that together determine how people typically behave in a society. Examples of rules are laws and regulations. In the context of property rights enforcement, rules define the relevant properties, assign property rights, define offences against property and specify corresponding (legal) penalties. It is important to realise that rules cannot themselves guarantee the conditions required for growth. Rules can be ignored. What matters is how the agents within an economy behave, and rules play a role only if they are adhered to in the main. Beliefs are also important here, because people are more inclined to obey a rule if they think that others will do likewise.

Consider now the part played by organisations such as the judicial system (courts and police) and corporations. A properly functioning judicial system administers sanctions to agents who flout the law and thus increases the probability that laws will be obeyed. But notice that this requires members of the judiciary themselves to behave in an appropriate manner. People must expect that the police will arrest offenders and that the courts will sentence criminals.

Turning now to business corporations, one important characteristic they have in developed economies is a legal identity and as such they can, just like an individual, own property, enter into contracts, sue and be sued. Moreover, the lifespan of a corporation is unlimited, unlike that of an individual. This fact enables a corporation to enter into longer-term contracts than would be possible for an individual and thus offers an increased potential for growth. As with the judicial system, the efficacy of a corporation in promoting growth does, of course, depend upon the behaviour of its members.

The fact that it is not the institutions as such, but rather the behaviour associated with them, that determines the growth potential of an economy suggests that the relationship between a country's institutional structure and growth is not a straightforward one. Moreover, institutions do not come from thin air. Although it is possible for institutions to spread from one country to another, current institutions are usually closely related to past ones. History matters.

Thus, for example, it has been argued that some of the key elements inherited from medieval institutions in Europe have played an important role in facilitating modern economic growth. Individualism, bodies of political representation and corporations with state-like authority were key features of an institutional system that supported increasingly complex and impersonal exchange.

Individualism, political representation and economic corporations — albeit without coercive power — have remained a central part of European economic institutions to the present day. It is interesting to note that these institutional elements were missing in the pre-modern histories of other great civilisations like China and the Muslim world. Even within Europe these medieval institutions did not extend everywhere. They were absent, for example, from much of eastern Europe, southern Italy, the Balkans and various parts of Spain. Note that these were the very areas that were late to industrialise. Similarly, many less developed countries have failed to develop their institutions along these lines in the post-colonial period.

It is clear that institutional reform is not straightforward and attempts to impose the West's 'best practices' have generally accomplished less than was hoped for. One reason is the major influence that existing institutional elements have on the direction and rate of institutional change.

The forms best fitted to achieving a particular outcome depend on the particularities of the country concerned and can differ from those currently prevailing in the West. The examples of the high-performing east Asian economies (Japan, South Korea and Taiwan) and the more recently booming China and India are examples of this point.

The Washington Consensus

The West's current 'best practices' — its rules and regulations — are called the Washington Consensus. They involve, among other things, deregulation, liberalisation of trade and financial systems and the privatisation of state enterprises. However, both South Korea's and Taiwan's growth policies exhibit significant departures from the Washington Consensus. Neither country undertook significant deregulation or liberalisation of their trade and financial systems until well into the 1980s and, far from privatising, they both relied heavily on public enterprises. An outside observer who knew the prescriptions of the Washington Consensus might well have concluded that South Korea, Taiwan — and Japan before them — stood little chance of developing.

The same applies to China's boom since the late 1970s and to India's less phenomenal, but still significant, growth since the early 1980s.

While both of these countries have transformed their attitudes towards markets and private enterprise during this period, their policy frameworks bear little resemblance to what is prescribed in the Washington Consensus. China, for example, took a totally different approach to reform — one that was experimental in nature and relied on a series of institutional innovations that departed significantly from Western norms.

It is important to realise that, in the end, these innovations delivered, for a couple of decades at least, the same goals that the Western economist would have been hoping for: market-oriented incentives, property rights, macroeconomic stability. But they

did so in a peculiar fashion that, given the Chinese historical and political context, had numerous advantages.

Conclusions

Institutions are a fundamental cause of long-run growth of per capita income. They are not merely rules and organisations, but rather a system of rules, beliefs, norms and organisations that support each other mutually and together generate regularities of social behaviour. Institutional reform is complicated by the fact that past institutional elements exert an influence on current institutions and that there is no one institutional structure appropriate for all countries in all periods.

Extract 4 Economic growth in developing countries

Overseas assistance

Overseas assistance (often simply known as 'aid') is composed of flows of funds from rich to poor countries on concessional terms. On the face of it this would seem to be a promising way of overcoming the savings gap and providing funds for investment. However, in practice aid does not seem to have fulfilled this promise.

One reason for this is that not all developing countries have been able to make good use of the funds provided by this route. According to the World Bank, this has been especially the case where countries have suffered from poor governance. For example, if a country suffers from macroeconomic instability or from a weak institutional structure, then aid funds may not be effective. There have also been some instances where aid has been siphoned off by corrupt officials, which clearly weakens the impact of aid by limiting the proportion of the funds that reach their intended destination.

It has also been the case in the past that some donor governments have seen overseas aid as part of trade policy, so that the granting of aid has been conditional on the recipient country using the funds to purchase goods from the donor country, sometimes at inflated prices.

Foreign direct investment

A second possibility for drawing in external funds is through foreign direct investment (FDI) by multinational corporations.

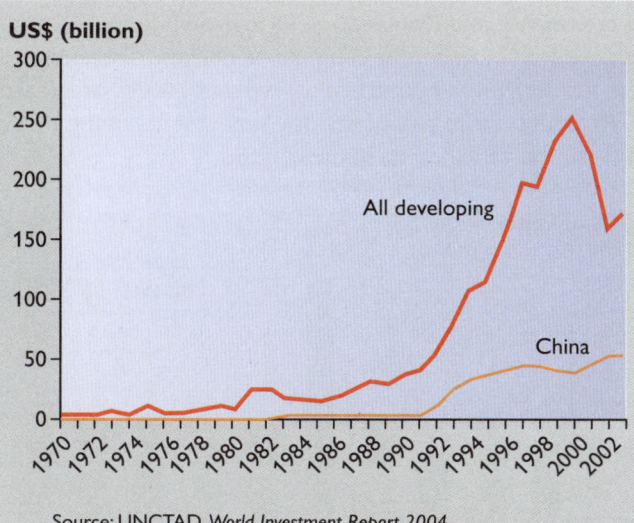

Source: UNCTAD, *World Investment Report 2004*

Figure 1 Foreign direct investment inflows, 1970–2003

Figure 1 shows inflows of FDI into developing countries since 1970. This illustrates clearly the increasing importance of FDI, especially during the late 1990s, although the flow appears to have been interrupted around the turn of the century, partly because of the 11 September terrorist attacks. The figure also shows that China has been a significant magnet for FDI since it began allowing foreign investment in the early 1990s.

In evaluating the effectiveness of FDI as a source of development funding, it is important to stay objective, as the topic has been contentious in recent years. In particular, the anti-globalisation lobby has criticised multinationals for exploiting the countries in which they have chosen to locate. These arguments have not always been strongly based on facts and we must therefore maintain a proper perspective on the debate.

On the positive side, FDI can be seen as a benefit, as the multinationals bring capital and technology, create jobs and have the experience needed to market their products in international markets. On the other hand, we must not lose sight of the fact that they are not humanitarian organisations, but companies seeking to maximise global after-tax profits. This will influence their behaviour.

International borrowing

The third way in which a developing country may obtain foreign funds for domestic investment is through borrowing on international capital markets. Borrowing can be effective, so long as the funds are used wisely and productively. In particular, it is important that the funds are used in such a way as to enable an increase in export earnings in the future, as a key aspect of borrowing is that debt must be repaid at some point. The debt situation of many developing countries came to worldwide attention in the late 1990s, when there was much pressure on creditor nations to allow debt relief for low-income countries which were perceived to be so crippled by

debt that they were unable to devote resources to growth and development. This was particularly the case for some countries in sub-Saharan Africa. Figure 2 shows debt service ratios for a selection of countries in 1990 and 2003. For example, in the case of Uganda in 1990, debt service payments (the repayments being made on past debt) were taking up more than 80% of the value of exports.

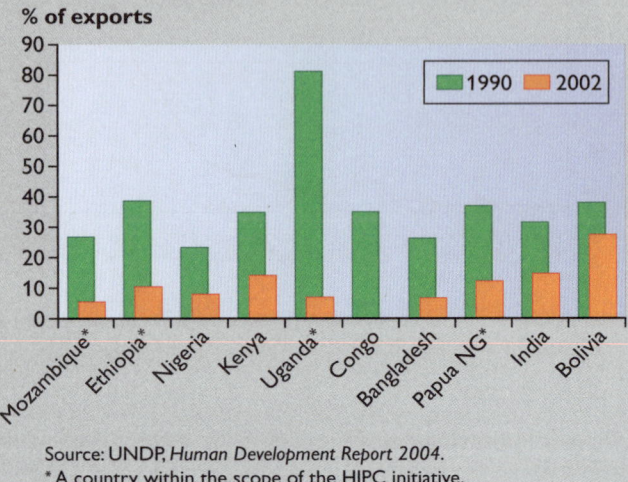

Source: UNDP, *Human Development Report 2004*.
* A country within the scope of the HIPC initiative.

Figure 2 Debt service in 1990 and 2002 (selected countries)

The heavily indebted poor countries initiative (HIPC), launched by the World Bank in 1995, set out to tackle the problem by awarding debt forgiveness to countries showing a commitment to sound economic policies and which implemented poverty reduction strategies. Since that time, there has been a significant reduction in the debt service burden for many countries, as you can see in Figure 2. However, it is not entirely clear whether this was directly connected to the HIPC initiative, as a number of countries witnessing a significant decline in debt burdens in this period were not part of the initiative (as shown in Figure 2). It is also important to realise that not all countries have seen their debt burden fall in this period. Indeed, the data indicate that for some countries (Burundi, Zambia and Belize), the debt burden increased appreciably between 1990 and 2002.

Extract 5 Economic development and the environment

Global warming

The sun's radiation reaches the Earth's surface in short wavelengths, but these are then transformed into long-wave, infrared bands when reflected back again. Certain gases in the Earth's atmosphere, along with water vapour, are penetrable to the short wavelength rays entering the atmosphere, but not to the longer wavelengths reflected back. Consequently, these latter waves are trapped within the atmosphere, thereby warming the Earth's surface temperature from an uninhabitable –18°C to 15°C, in which life can exist. This process is very much like that inside a greenhouse — hence the terms 'greenhouse effect' and the 'greenhouse gases' (the most significant of which is carbon dioxide — CO_2).

This is the natural element of the process, but humans have been increasingly adding to the greenhouse gas concentrations in the atmosphere, mainly through the burning of fossil fuels (man-made emissions are called anthropogenic emissions). This has been true especially since 1850 and the onset of the Industrial Revolution (Figure 1). By doing this, we are increasing the amount of waves that are trapped within the atmosphere, thereby increasing the Earth's surface temperature even more. It is this global warming that is the cause of so much concern at present.

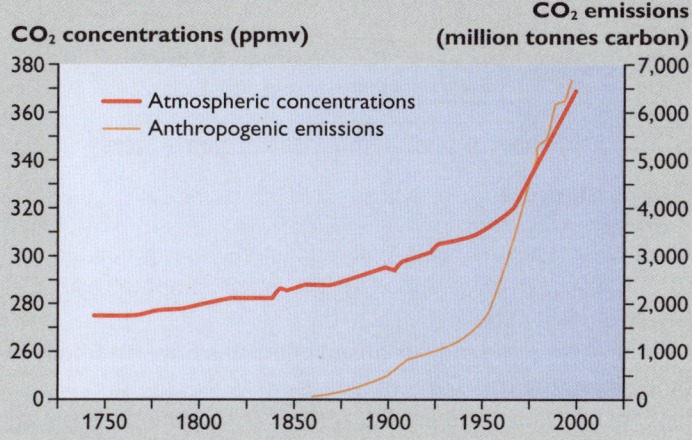

Figure 1 Carbon dioxide concentrations/emissions, 1750–2000

The intergovernmental panel on climate change (IPCC 1990) has estimated that a doubling of carbon dioxide in the atmosphere will increase the global mean temperature by approximately 2.5°C; and that if business continues as usual, this will be achieved by the year 2025. Cline (1991) has argued, however, that a longer time-span needs to be considered, because carbon dioxide remains active in the atmosphere for over two centuries. He has estimated that, by 2275, the level of carbon dioxide will have risen eight-fold compared to pre-industrial times, causing an increase in the Earth's temperature of nearer to 10°C.

The potential effects of this warming are wide-reaching, including:
- the sea level rising by approximately 66 cm from 1990 to 2100. A rise of 1 metre would eliminate 3% of the Earth's land area and an even larger proportion of its crop area (IPCC 2000)
- large ecosystem change, with the US Environmental Protection Agency predicting large-scale losses of forest and biodiversity
- serious weather effects. Emanuel (1989) has calculated that a doubling of carbon dioxide would cause the destructive power of hurricanes to increase by up to 50%, along with their regularity

Global warming and the environmental transition

Is global warming consistent with the environmental transition? It is certainly true that the predicted growth of carbon dioxide is greatest in developing countries, where emissions are expected to increase by 2.7% annually over the period 2001–25. This is shown in Figure 2.

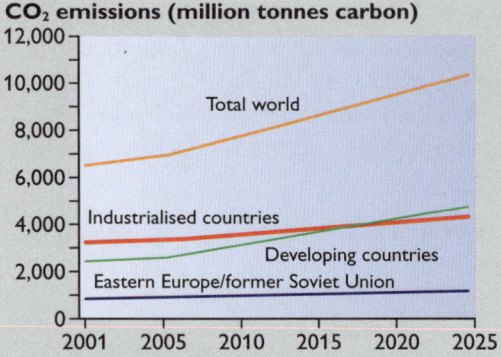

Figure 2 Predicted emissions of carbon dioxide

However, Figure 2 reveals as well that emissions are predicted to rise in the industrialised countries. In the context of the environmental transition argument there are, then, two possibilities:

- The first is that not even the industrialised countries have attained the level of per capita income where the transition occurs.
- The second is that the environmental transition argument does not apply to global warming.

The problem with the first argument is that, in terms of the nature of the damage caused, global warming is not dissimilar from other forms of environmental degradation, and thus it is not obvious why the income thresholds should be significantly different from the estimates reported above. However, in terms of the *source* of the damage, carbon dioxide emissions are fundamentally different from the types of pollution considered by Antle and Heidebrink and Grossman and Krueger — the difference being that carbon dioxide pollution transcends national boundaries.

Conclusions

Most people would agree that poorer countries should be helped to develop and grow, so that they can attain the freedoms and standard of living that are enjoyed in the industrialised world. But what are the implications for the quality of the environment?

We have argued that, while at low levels of development rising incomes are likely to lead to a deterioration in environmental quality, beyond some income threshold this process may be reversed, so that further development leads to improvements in some environment variables.

However, if such an 'environmental transition' applies to global warming, it is at the global, rather than the national, level. An individual country cannot significantly influence its exposure to global warming by controlling its own carbon dioxide emissions and thus the solution to the problem lies with decisions and actions taken at the international level.

Paper 3 **questions**

Time allowed: 2 hours

A clean copy of the pre-issued stimulus material is included with the question paper. Answer all questions. You will be assessed on the quality of written communication in question 3.

Total marks allocated: 60

(1) (a) Explain the economic cycle.   (4 marks)

ⓔ Note that there are only 4 marks available and do not get carried away with writing too much. A brief sentence on each of the phases of the cycle is sufficient.

(b) Analyse the multiplier and the accelerator.   (6 marks)

ⓔ These two concepts are often confused — remember that there is a multiplier effect on national income of a change in withdrawals or injections, and that there is an accelerator effect on investment caused by an increase in national income.

(c) Comment on the extent to which the multiplier and accelerator are causes of the economic cycle.   (10 marks)

ⓔ Because this is a 'to what extent' question, you must show awareness of a number of causes, not just the possible effect of the multiplier and the accelerator.

(2) (a) Distinguish between economic growth and sustainable economic growth.   (4 marks)

ⓔ It is not necessary to include a diagram in this answer, but it can be used to enhance the answer and reduce the amount that needs to be written to achieve full marks.

(b) Is foreign direct investment or international borrowing the more efficient way to promote development in a less developed country?   (6 marks)

ⓔ This question does require an answer that concludes whether it is FDI or international borrowing that is the more efficient and a final mark will be held back if no judgement is forthcoming.

(c) **Are the institutions within a country a fundamental cause of a long-run growth in per capita income?** (10 marks)

    ⓔ Extract 3 gives a clear indication of what is meant by institutions and your judgement is required as to whether they are a fundamental cause.

(3*) **Discuss whether the process of globalisation is likely to benefit the world economy.** (20 marks)

    ⓔ Because this is a discussion question, it is not sufficient to write only about the benefits of globalisation. Whether globalisation benefits the world economy requires a balanced look at the downside of the process. Also, although you may show awareness of what is meant by and what causes globalisation as you set the scene for your answer, these points are not specifically required by the wording of the question. However, you do need to refer to economic theory and the extent to which it applies in reality.

Mark scheme

(1) (a) In order to achieve 4 marks, it is necessary to explain the four phases of the cycle, i.e. boom, recession, depression and recovery. (4 marks)

    (b) The multiplier needs to be looked at from the point of view that a change in the injections into or withdrawals from the circular flow of income will have a multiple effect on national income (3 marks), while the accelerator is a response to a change in national income that will increase the rate of investment and accelerate the rate of growth of national income (3 marks).

    (c) First of all, provide an explanation of how the multiplier and accelerator produce an increase or a decrease either side of the trend rate of growth in GDP, often referred to as Keynesian theories. To complete the answer, it is necessary to determine whether this is the only cause of fluctuations in economic activity, or whether there are other possible causes such as:
- theories of over-production
- theories of under-consumption
- theories relating to business confidence
- monetary theories
- election cycle theories

Without showing awareness of other possible causes, a mark ceiling of 6 marks would be imposed. Some attempt at dealing with 'the extent' will open up the full range of 10 marks. (10 marks)

(2) (a) To achieve full marks, it is necessary to show that, by definition, economic growth can occur in a sustainable way or a non-sustainable way. For example, increased use of non-renewable resources could raise productive capacity per capita in the present, but would obviously not be sustainable into the future as resources are depleted. (4 marks)

    (b) It is important to show an understanding of the difference between FDI and international borrowing to promote growth. FDI by multinational firms brings expertise to countries and creates fixed capital and jobs, but it is likely to repatriate profits. In contrast, international borrowing can be used to build factories, promote jobs and make profits that can be used domestically and will also be needed to pay interest on the loans. It is likely that a conclusion based upon historical evidence will favour FDI, but a good argument can be put forward to support international borrowing. (6 marks)

(c) Long-run growth in per capita income will result from economic growth. Whether an economy grows is dependent upon many factors such as invention, innovation, and improvements in both human and non-human capital. In addition to this, the question is asking whether the political and judicial system in a country are necessary prerequisites that allow the other factors to promote growth. In the past a comparison has been made between growth rates in capitalist and command economies and it seems that economies with private property rights and the profit motive have grown at faster rates. This does not, however, mean that growth rates are highest in countries with identical institutions. Over recent years, Russia, India and China have all grown very fast; India and Russia based their political structure on democracy, whereas China remained an authoritarian society. The similarity in all cases was that they started to pursue a mixed economy with a significant proportion of total output produced under a capitalist banner. Extracts 2 and 3 will provide information and the answer needs to evaluate this question in order to achieve the full marks. (10 marks)

(3) To answer this question in a balanced way, it will be necessary to look at the benefits and costs of globalisation and set out the answer in an essay style where an introduction will explain the process of globalisation, a conclusion will perhaps look at this in the context of the current economic climate and the main part of the answer will look at the benefits:

• globalisation is likely to promote economic growth and development
• it provides an opportunity to raise people from poverty without making others worse off
• improved transportation and communication will contribute to lower unit costs of production
• larger markets can improve the quality of products and allow a fuller utilisation of economies of scale
• lowering of trade barriers can allow the theory of comparative advantage to produce specialisation and gains from trade
• it makes a greater variety of products available for customers to choose from
• it provides an opportunity to solve environmental problems as income thresholds are crossed

and the costs:

• opportunity costs arise in the pursuit of growth and development policies
• there are personal costs involved in having to adapt to a rapidly changing world
• social costs of increased consumption and production, e.g. pollution and global warming, can arise
• there is a lack of international rules, regulations and laws to promote a level playing field and competitive free markets
• it can cause greater conflict between different cultures and religious groups (20 marks)

A-grade answer

(I) (a) This is sometimes known as the business cycle, which can be regular or irregular, when the economy passes through a number of stages. If we start with a boom — which is characterised by high incomes, rising prices and high levels of employment — then this is followed by a recession when unemployment starts to rise and growth slows. At the bottom of the cycle this may lead to a depression or slump, when unemployment is high and growth may be negative and deflation may occur. As things start to get better, the economy goes through a recovery phase where economic indicators begin to improve back towards a boom.

ⓔ **4/4 marks awarded.** Each phase of the cycle is sufficiently well explained to achieve full marks.

(b) If there is an injection into the circular flow of income then real GDP may rise by a factor greater than the original injection. This is illustrated in the diagram below, where the change in Y divided by the change in J gives a multiplier value.

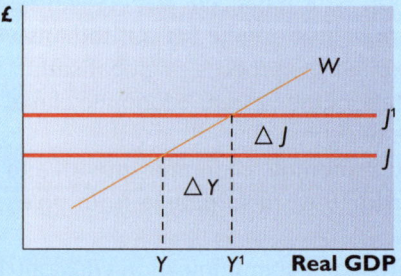

The change in national income will also boost investment, which will give a further boost to the national income. It is assumed that, in order to maintain the same capital–output ratio, a sudden increase in national income will cause an accelerator effect. This is because, for one period of time, it will be both necessary to replace worn out capital and to buy new capital.

ⓔ **4/6 marks awarded.** The student understands both concepts, but the analysis is fairly descriptive and does not include algebraic formulations of both concepts or a recognition of a possible downward multiplier effect.

(c) The multiplier and the accelerator can be linked over time in a way that might explain the movement towards a boom. If the multiplier effect of an injection into the economy is followed by the accelerator effect on investment, then the combined effect may move the economy above its trend growth rate. Also in a downturn, an increase in withdrawals from the circular flow of income will have an effect which is greater than the original change and bring the economy below trend. The Keynesian interpretation of the economic cycle focuses on these combined effects.

However, there are other potential causes. An unexpected economic event may cause consumer demand to shrink and start off a cycle of under-consumption, or, alternatively, over-production may occur in an economy. Particularly at risk are economies where agricultural output is a large proportion of total output; its variable nature may put the cycle into motion.

Another cluster of theories is concerned with psychology and business confidence. Events such as 9/11 or the collapse of Lehman Brothers may destroy confidence and a recession may set in just because it was thought likely to happen.

Monetarist economists have put forward the idea that unexpected expansions or contractions in the money supply could start off an economic cycle. Some economists have gone further and linked this to an election cycle where over-exuberant politicians push for expansion before an election and then have to hold back afterwards. This has been referred to as the stop–go cycle.

🅮 **8/10 marks awarded.** This answer shows awareness of different causes of the economic cycle as well as explaining a possible role for the multiplier and accelerator.

(2) (a) An economy grows when there is an increase in its productive capacity per capita and the production possibility boundary shifts outward from AA to BB, as shown in the diagram below:

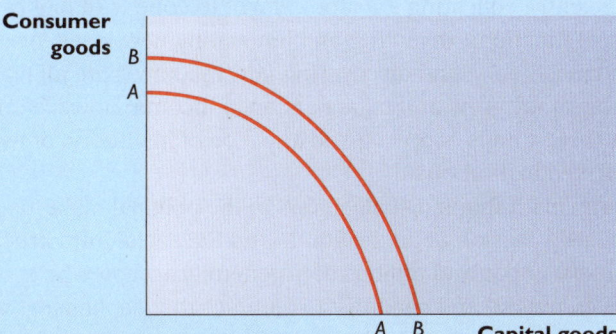

This can occur in a number of ways and they may be sustainable or not. For example, growing by using up a finite amount of non-renewable resources is not sustainable, whereas educating the workforce more efficiently is sustainable. Sustainability requires the economy to grow in a way that will not compromise the next generation's standard of living.

🅮 **4/4 marks awarded.** The student understands the difference and supports the answer with examples.

(b) Foreign direct investment is when multinational companies invest directly in a foreign country. It has been a significant source of investment in less developed countries, particularly when firms have out-sourced their manufacturing to places with low labour costs. It has met with criticism in as much as people have accused MNCs of exploiting distressed countries and destroying jobs in their own countries. Another source of funding, particularly for less developed countries, is borrowing from more developed countries. This has the advantage of allowing money to be used to invest in one's own country, but has the disadvantage that it may not be invested as efficiently.

International borrowing requires interest payments to be serviced and debt to be repaid, but what is left will be owned domestically. FDI will employ people locally, raise income and provide skills, but ownership will be in a foreign country and profits may be repatriated rather than used locally. The evidence that has been collected seems to suggest that, despite the criticism, FDI has brought about a more efficient allocation of resources than has international borrowing.

ⓔ **5/6 marks awarded.** There are some good points of argument and the student answers the question.

(c) There are many reasons why an economy undergoes a process of economic growth. Taking the resources currently being used and reorganising them more efficiently, educating the labour force to cope with higher-order intellectual functions, inventing and innovating new ideas, investing in new plant and machinery, and discovering new resources are all ways in which an economy may grow and raise per capita income. However, the question is whether these things happen given any type of institution or even with a lack of established institutions.

The term 'institutions' usually refers to the political make-up of a country, including its provision of public goods and the social infrastructure that may include merit goods and utilities. It is generally accepted by economists who compare command and capitalist economies that capitalism, with its private property rights and profit motive, is likely to promote growth, whereas the lack of motivation and reward in a command economy tends to hold it back.

Today, capitalism in an economic sense can exist with or without democracy, and countries like China have shown considerable rates of growth without having a democratic political structure. Stability and confidence in institutions is also seen to be important if an economy is to grow.

In answering the question regarding whether the institutions are a fundamental cause of a long-run growth in per capita income, the answer is probably no — but it seems to be the case that they are important in allowing the other factors that cause growth to function efficiently.

ⓔ **7/10 marks awarded.** The student shows a good understanding of the question and attempts an answer, although things could have been explained in a little more depth.

(3) The process of globalisation is taking place as the flows of people, products, money and ideas increase around the world. It is occurring as the result of reduced transport costs (economy airlines), reduced communication costs (free internet), reductions in trade barriers, an increase in multinational companies and the deregulation of financial markets.

Globalisation makes it possible for the theory of comparative advantage to bring about specialisation across the world. Firms can enter new markets and expand to take advantage of economies of scale and there should be gains from trade for all. If the world economy grows then its citizens will become better off without the requirement of redistributive policies. Even if redistributive policies are used to alleviate poverty, it is just that the poor can get an increased share of the growth in output, again without taking it away from anyone else.

Increased flows of people around the world will tend to equalise incomes. Those who move in search of higher incomes will tend to have a depressing effect on high incomes as there is an increase in supply, while the places they move from will have a reduction in labour supply that will tend to raise wage rates.

Intolerance and conflict often take place between countries through ignorance, and these impose economic costs. Arguably, greater communication and awareness throughout the world may reduce this intolerance and conflict and therefore have an economic benefit on the world economy.

The economic growth and development aspect of globalisation will allow people to increase their leisure time and also to raise their standard of living. Successive generations will have their increased expectations of higher standards of living fulfilled and the current generation of people will further their aspirations of becoming better off in their own lifetime.

Globalisation makes people aware of, and may be a further cause of, environmental degradation. However, the rise in real incomes across the world, when it has passed a certain threshold, may make it easier to deal with these problems.

The effects of economic growth and development through globalisation will not necessarily be immediate. There is an opportunity cost when resources are allocated to investment, which is that they cannot be allocated to consumption. Immediate standards of living thereby become lower in the present than they need be but hopefully they will improve considerably in the future.

A potentially damaging group of costs to the world economy is external costs. Greater consumption of products, such as cars and air travel, will increase the risk of global warming and air pollution, while greater production will use up non-renewable resources, cause more air and water pollution and increase environmental degradation. These problems may accelerate over the next few years as it is the world's largest countries by population size, e.g. China and India, which are growing the fastest.

There will also be considerable personal costs to individuals across the world as they find things rapidly changing and they have to become geographically and occupationally more mobile. Also the faster the world changes, the more people may be affected by unpleasant breaks in their working lives. In addition, as the world gets more closely interactive so a relatively small problem in one part of the

world may have knock-on effects across the whole world. For example, a localised sub-prime lending problem in America has been blamed for causing a global meltdown as one bank after another struggles to survive and all the companies linked to those banks across the world feel the impact.

There are many potential benefits from globalisation but there are also many risks. Greater knowledge and easier communication may exacerbate global conflict by bringing small dissident groups together to create a real global terrorist problem. Also the current credit crunch may cause globalisation to go into reverse as countries start to raise economic barriers in an attempt to isolate themselves from global problems.

e 17/20 marks awarded. This is a well-balanced answer that has the added advantage of making use of up-to-date information that is not in the textbooks and therefore shows clear evidence of wider reading in current journals. The mark allocation is 13 for content and 4 for the quality of written communication.

e Scored 49/60 = 81.7% = Grade A

Knowledge check answers

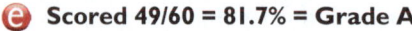

1 Absolute advantage exists when more products can be produced using the same amount of resources, while comparative advantage can exist in the absence of absolute advantage as long as the opportunity costs of production are different between competitors.

2 More capital goods means more investment and this is almost always a prerequisite of an increase in the productive capacity per capita of an economy.

3 By the average price level falling from AP to AP^1.

4 The opportunity cost of forgoing consumption when investing in economic growth. Also there will be personal costs to individuals and external costs to society.

5 Any table that produces the same opportunity costs does not illustrate any comparative advantage. For example, if the two numbers for A are 50 and 30 and for B they are 25 and 15 then opportunity costs must be the same.

6 PPP is £1 =$2. You must ignore the exchange rate.

7 Their unit costs of production are significantly higher than their more mature competitors as they have not yet grown to a size that can take full advantage of economies of scale. Therefore they cannot initially compete in a free and open market but hopefully will when they reach an optimum size.

8 Imports rise in price and exports fall in price.

9 Appreciation is likely to make the situation worse so you would choose to deflate domestic demand. This will reduce the demand for imports and release resources to be directed towards the export market.

10 It is a collection of firms that extract raw materials from natural sources. These raw materials can then be used in the manufacture of goods and the provision of services.

11 Standard of living includes quantifiable characteristics such as goods and services consumed, but also unquantifiable things such as low levels of stress, pleasant climate, nice scenery, political stability and many other factors.

12 The main difference is that the World Bank's main objective is to assist in economic development through loans for capital investment on reasonable terms, while the IMF oversees exchange rate policies and currency problems that may be contingent upon accepting prescribed austerity measures.

Page numbers in **bold** refer to **key term definitions**

Index